Guitar Chord Songbook

Motown

ISBN-13: 978-1-4234-0099-8
ISBN-10: 1-4234-0099-2

HAL•LEONARD®
CORPORATION
7777 W. BLUEMOUND RD. P.O. BOX 13819 MILWAUKEE, WI 53213

Visit Hal Leonard Online at
www.halleonard.com

Contents

ABC

Words and Music by
Alphonso Mizell, Frederick Perren,
Deke Richards and Berry Gordy

Melody:

You went to school to learn __ girl,

A   D

| *Intro* | | A   D | A   D | |

| *Verse 1* | A   D |

You went to school to learn girl,

A   D

Things you never, never knew be - fore.

A   D

Like I before E ex - cept after C.

A   D

And why two plus two makes four.

A   D

Now, now, now, I'm going to teach you. (Teach you, teach you.)

A   D

All about love, dear. (All about love.)

A   D

Sit yourself down, take a seat

A   D

All you gotta do is re - peat after me.

Chorus 1

   A   D   A   D
A, B, C,   easy as 1, 2, 3.

                A   D
Ah, simple as Do, Re, Mi, A, B, C

   A   D
1, 2, 3 Baby, you and me, girl.

   A   D   A   D
A, B, C,   easy as 1, 2, 3.

                A   D
Ah, simple as Do, Re, Mi, A, B, C

   A   D   A
1, 2, 3 baby, you and me, girl.

Bridge 1

   A
Come on, let me love you just a little bit!

Come on, let me love you just a little bit!

I'm a going to teach how to sing it out!

Come on, come on, come on

Let me show you what it's all about!

Verse 2

   A   D
Reading and writing, 'rithmetic

        A   D
Are the branches of the learning tree.

            A   D
But listen, with - out the roots of love ev'ryday girl,

       A   D
Your education ain't com - plete.

       A   D
T-t-t- teachers gonna show you (Show you, show you.)

   A   D
How to get an "A." (Na, na, na, na, na, na.)

       A   D
Spell me, you   add the two.

   A   D
Listen to me baby, that's all you gotta do.

Chorus 2

       A   D   A   D
Oh, A, B, C,   it's easy as 1, 2, 3.

              A   D
Ah, simple as Do, Re, Mi, A, B, C

A   D
1, 2, 3 baby, you and me, girl.

A   D   A   D
A, B, C, it's easy, it's like counting up to three.

       A   D A   D
Sing a simple melo - dy, that's how easy love can be.

A   D
That's how easy love can be.

A   D   A   D   N.C.
Sing a simple melody, 1, 2, 3, you and me.

Bridge 2

N.C.
Yah! Sit down girl, I think I love you!

No, get up, girl!

Show me what you can do!

A   D
Shake it, shake it, baby, come on now!

A   D
Shake it, shake it baby, ooh, ooh.

A   D
Shake it, shake it, baby, huh!

A   D
1, 2, 3 baby, ooh, ooh.

A   D
A, B, C baby, na, na.

A   D
Do, re, mi baby, huh!

A   D
That's how easy love can be.

Chorus 3

  A   D   A   D
A, B, C, it's easy, it's like counting up to three.

   A   D A   D A
Sing a simple melo - dy, that's how easy love can be.

I'm a gonna teach you how to sing it out.

Come-a, come-a, come-a, let me show you what it's all about.

A   D   A   D
A, B, C, it's easy, it's like counting up to three.

   A   D A   D A
Sing a simple melo - dy, that's how easy love can be.

I'm a gonna teach you how to sing it out,

Sing it out, sing it out, baby, baby.

Outro   *Repeat Chorus 3 till fade*

Ain't No Mountain High Enough

Words and Music by Nickolas Ashford
and Valerie Simpson

Melody:

Lis - ten ba - by.   Ain't no moun-tain _ high

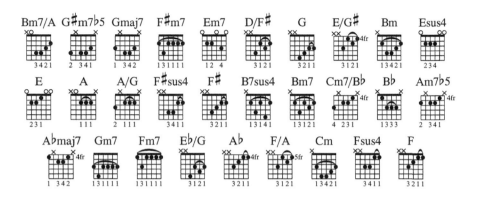

Intro |Bm7/A G#m7b5| |Gmaj7 F#m7 Em7 |D/F# G E/G#
                                               Male: Listen, ba - by.

    Bm7/A   G#m7b5   Gmaj7
    Ain't no mountain high, ain't no valley low,

          F#m7   Em7   D/F# G E/G#
    Ain't no river wide ___ enough ___ ba - by.

          Bm7/A   G#m7b5   Gmaj7
Verse 1   *Female:*   If you need me call me no matter where you are

         F#m7 Em7   D/F# G   E/G# Bm7/A
    No matter how far. *Male:* Don't worry, ba   -   by.

           G#m7b5   Gmaj7
    Female: Just call my name, I'll be there in a hur - ry

       F#m7   Em7
    You don't have to worry

Chorus 1

F#m7   Gmaj7 Em7   F#m7 Bm
Both: 'Cause baby there ain't no mountain high e - nough,

Gmaj7 Em7 F#m7 Bm
Ain't no valley low e - nough,

Gmaj7 Em7 F#m7 Bm
Ain't no river wide e - nough

Esus4   E   G
To keep me from getting to you, babe.

Verse 2

Bm7/A   G#m7♭5
Male: Remember the day I set you free?

Gmaj7 F#m7 Em7
I told you you could always count on me, darlin'.

D/F#   G E/G# Bm7/A
From that day on, _____

G#m7♭5   Gmaj7
I made a vow; I'll be there when you want me,

F#m7   Em7
Some - way some - how.

Chorus 2

Repeat Chorus 1

Bridge

A
Male: Oh no, darling.

A/G F#sus4 F#
Female: No wind, no rain ___ or winter's cold

B7sus4 Bm7   Gmaj7
Can stop me, ba - by. *Male:* No, no baby.

Bm7/A A   Bm7/A   A
If you're ever in trouble, I'll be there on the double.

Cm7/B♭ B♭
Just send for me. *Both:* Oh baby.

Verse 3

       Cm7/B♭   Am7♭5   A♭maj7
Female: Oh, my love is a - live deep down in my heart,

   Gm7   Fm7
Al - though we are miles apart.

   E♭/G A♭ F/A Cm7/B♭ Am7♭5
Male: If you ev - er need a helping hand,

        A♭maj7 Gm7 Fm7
I'll be there on the dou - ble just as fast as I can.

Chorus 3

       Gm7   A♭maj7 Fm7 Gm7 Cm
Both: Don't you know that there ain't no mountain high e - nough,

A♭maj7 Fm7 Gm7 Cm
Ain't no valley low e - nough,

A♭maj7 Fm7 Gm7 Cm
Ain't no river wide e - nough

 Fsus4   F   A♭
To keep me from getting to you, babe.

Chorus 4

         A♭maj7 Fm7 Gm7 Cm
Both: Don't you know that there ain't no mountain high e - nough,

A♭maj7 Fm7 Gm7 Cm
Ain't no valley low e - nough,

A♭maj7 Fm7 Gm7 Cm
Ain't no river wide e - nough,

A♭maj7 Fm7 Gm7 Cm
Ain't no mountain high e - nough

A♭maj7 Fm7 Gm7 Cm
Ain't no valley low e - nough. *Fade out*

Ain't Too Proud to Beg

Words and Music by Edward Holland
and Norman Whitfield

I know _ you wan-na leave me,

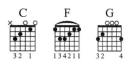

Verse 1

N.C. (C)
I know you wanna leave me,

  F   C
    But I re - fuse to let you go.

  F   C
If I have to beg, plead for your sympathy,

  F   C
I don't mind 'cause you mean that much to me.

Chorus 1

N.C.(G)   C   F   C
Ain't too proud to beg,   and you know it.

  F   C   F   C
Please don't leave ___ me, girl. (Don't you go.)

      F   C   F   C
Ain't too proud to plead, baby, ba - by.

  F   C   F   C
Please don't leave ___ me, girl. (Don't you go.)

Verse 2

    F   **C N.C.**
    Now, I've heard a cryin' man is half a man,

    C N.C.
With no sense of pride.

        C N.C.
But if I have to cry to keep you, I don't mind weepin'

    C N.C.   **G**
If it'll keep you by my side.

Chorus 2

        C   **F**   **C**
Ain't too proud to beg,   sweet dar - lin',

F   **C**   **F**   **C**
Please don't leave ___ me, girl. (Don't you go.)

   F   **C** **F**   **C**
Ain't too proud to plead, baby, ba - by.

F   **C**   **F**   **C**
Please don't leave ___ me, girl. (Don't you go.)

Verse 3

    F   **C N.C.**
If I have to sleep on your doorstep all night and day

    C N.C.
Just to keep you from walking away.

    C N.C.
Let your friends laugh, even this I can stand,

    C N.C.   **G**
'Cause I wanna keep you anyway I can,

Chorus 3

```
        C          F            C
Ain't too proud to beg, sweet dar - lin',

F              C            F        C
Please don't leave ___ me, girl. (Don't you go.)

      F         C   F      C
Ain't too proud to plead, baby, ba - by.

F              C            F        G
Please don't leave ___ me, girl. (Don't you go.)
```

Sax Solo

```
‖: C      F     C  |            F    :‖  Play 3 times
|  C      F        | G                |
```

Verse 4

```
                 C N.C.
Now, I've got a love so deep in the pit of my heart,

            C N.C.
And each day it grows more and more.

            C N.C.
I'm not a - shamed to call and plea to you, baby,

        C N.C.              G
If pleading keeps you from walkin' out that door.
```

Chorus 4

Repeat Chorus 3

Outro

```
F          C    F       C      F      F C
Baby, baby, baby.   Sweet darlin'.  Ooh.     Fade out
```

Ain't Nothing Like the Real Thing

Words and Music by Nickolas Ashford
and Valerie Simpson

Melody:

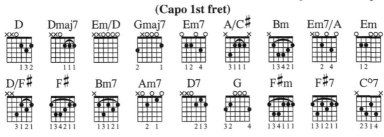

Ain't noth-ing like the real thing, ba - by.

(Capo 1st fret)

D   Dmaj7   Em/D   Gmaj7   Em7   A/C#   Bm   Em7/A   Em

D/F#   F#   Bm7   Am7   D7   G   F#m   F#7   C°7

Intro

    D
Ooh, baby.

Chorus 1

                 Dmaj7   **Em/D D Em/D D**
Male: Female: Ain't nothing like the real   thing, ba - by.

    Gmaj7   **Em7**   **D**
    Ain't nothing like the real thing. *Male:* No, no.

            Dmaj7   **Em/D D**   **Em/D D**
Both: Ain't nothing like the real   thing, ba - by.

    Gmaj7   **Em7**
    Ain't nothing like the real thing.

           D A/C# Bm
Male: No, hon - ey.

Verse 1

             Em7/A D   **Em**   **D/F#**
Female: I've got your picture hangin' on the wall,

    Gmaj7   **F#**   **Bm7**
    But it can't see or come to me when I call your name.

    Am7 D7   **G**   **D**
    I realize ____ it's just a picture in a frame.

                       Em   **D/F#**
Male: Ooh, I read your letters when you're not near,

    Gmaj7   **F#**
    But they don't move me and they don't groove me

    Bm7   **Am7**   **G**   **D**
    Like when I hear your sweet voice whispering in my ear.

Chorus 2

Female: Don't you know,

            Dmaj7   Em/D D   Em/D D
Both: Ain't nothing like the real   thing, ba - by.

Gmaj7   Em7
  Ain't nothing like the real thing.

Verse 2

               D   Em D/F$\sharp$
Female: I play my game, a fantasy.

Gmaj7   F$\sharp$ Bm7
I pretend, but I know in re - ality

 Am7   D7   G   D
I need the shelter of your arms to comfort me.

        F$\sharp$m   F$\sharp$7   Bm
Both: No other sound is quite the same as your name.

 D7   G   D   C°7
No touch can do half as much   *Male:* to make me feel better.

     Em7   Em7/A
Female: So, let's stay to - gether.

Verse 3

               D   Em   D/F$\sharp$
Male: I've got some mem'ries to look back on.

Gmaj7   F$\sharp$
Though they help me when you phone,

 Bm7   Am7
I'm well aware nothing can

G   D
Take the place of your being there.

Chorus 3

            Dmaj7   Em/D D   Em/D D
Both: Oh, so glad we got the the real   thing, ba - by.

Gmaj7   Em7
  So glad we got the real thing.

Outro

       D   Dmaj7   Em/D D   Em/D D
Both: ‖: Ain't nothing like the real   thing, ba - by.

Gmaj7   Em7
  Ain't nothing like the real thing.   :‖ *Repeat and fade*

Baby I Need Your Lovin'

Words and Music by Brian Holland,
Lamont Dozier and Edward Holland

Ba - by, I ____ need __ your __ lov - in'.

(Capo 1st fret)

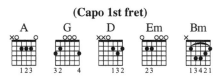

| | A | G | D | Em | Bm |

Intro

    A   G   D
‖: Ooh, ooh, ooh. :‖ *Play 3 times*

Verse 1

A   D
Baby, I need your lovin'.

A   D
Baby, I need your lovin'.

A   D
Although you're ____ never near,

A   D
Your voice I ____ often hear.

A   D
Another day, 'nother night,

A   D
I long ____ to hold you tight,

A   D
'Cause I'm so lonely.

Chorus 1

G   Em
Baby, I need ____ your lovin'.

D   Bm
Got to have all ____ your lovin'.

G   Em
Baby, I need ____ your lovin'.

D   Bm
Got to have all ____ your lovin'.

Verse 2

> A   D
> Some say ____ it's a sign of weakness
>
> A   D
> For a man ____ to beg.
>
> A   D
> Then weak I'd ____ rather be,
>
> A   D
> If it means hav - ing you to keep,
>
> A   D
> 'Cause lately I've been losing sleep.

Chorus 2

Repeat Chorus 1

Verse 3

> A   G A G A
> Empty nights ____ echo your name.
>
> G A   G A
> Oh, sometimes ____ I wonder
>
> G   D A G D
> Will I ever be the same?
>
> A   D
> When you see me smil - ing,
>
>   A   D
> You know things ____ have gotten worse.
>
> A   D
> Any smile you might see
>
> A   D
> Has all ____ been rehearsed.
>
> A   D   G D
> Darlin', I ____ can't go on without you.
>
> A   D   A G
> This emptiness won't let me live without you.
>
> A   D   A G
> This loneliness inside me, darlin',
>
> A   D
> Makes me feel half alive.

Chorus 3

Repeat Chorus 1

Outro

>   G   Em
> ‖: Baby, I need ____ your lovin'.
>
> D   Bm
> Got to have all ____ your lovin'. :‖ *Repeat and fade*

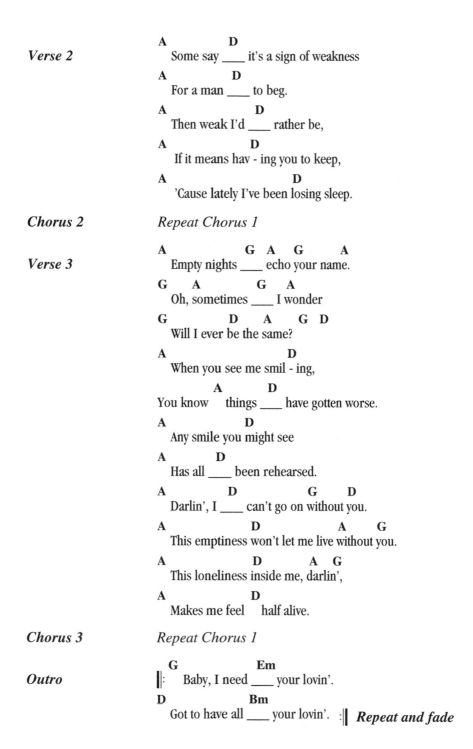

Baby Love

Words and Music by Brian Holland,
Edward Holland and Lamont Dozier

Melody:

Ba - by love ___ my ba - by love, ___

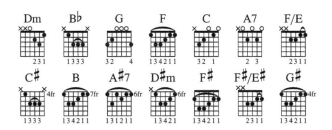

Dm   Bb   G   F   C   A7   F/E

C#   B   A#7   D#m   F#   F#/E#   G#

Intro |Dm |Bb |G   F |C N.C. |

Verse 1

               C   Bb
Ooh, ooh ba - by love, my baby love,

     A7   Dm
I need you, oh how I need you.

               C
But all you do is treat me bad,

    F   C
Break my heart and leave me sad.

    F   C
Tell me, what did I do wrong

      F   F/E   Dm   G
To make you stay a - way so long?

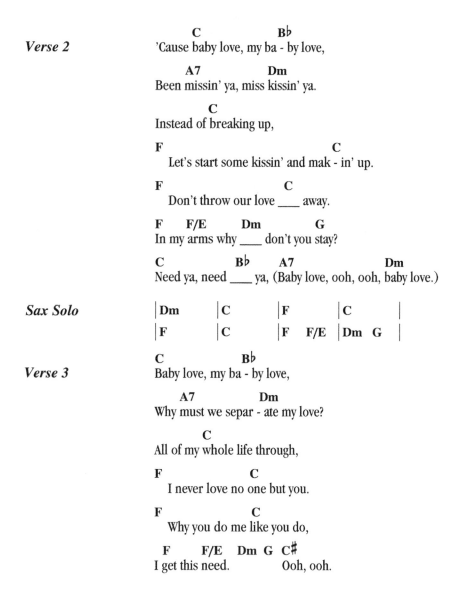

Verse 2

          C   Bb
'Cause baby love, my ba - by love,

          A7   Dm
Been missin' ya, miss kissin' ya.

          C
Instead of breaking up,

F   C
  Let's start some kissin' and mak - in' up.

F   C
  Don't throw our love ___ away.

F   F/E   Dm   G
In my arms why ___ don't you stay?

C   Bb   A7   Dm
Need ya, need ___ ya, (Baby love, ooh, ooh, baby love.)

Sax Solo

| Dm | C | F | C | |
| F | C | F F/E | Dm G | |

Verse 3

C   Bb
Baby love, my ba - by love,

          A7   Dm
Why must we separ - ate my love?

          C
All of my whole life through,

F   C
  I never love no one but you.

F   C
  Why you do me like you do,

  F   F/E   Dm G C#
I get this need.   Ooh, ooh.

Verse 4

        C#   B
Need to hold you once a - gain my love,

        A#7   D#m
Feel your warm embrace ____ my love.

            C#
Don't throw our love away,

F#   C#
  Please don't do me this way.

F#   C#
  Not happy like I used to be,

F#   F#/E# D#m G#
Loneli - ness has got the best of me.

Verse 5

C#   B
My love, my baby love,

  A#7   D#m
I need ya, oh how I need you.

          C#
Why you do me like you do,

F#   C#
  After I've been true to you.

F#   C#
  So deep in love with you,

F#   F#/E# D#m G#
Baby, baby,   ooh.

        C#   B
Till it's hurtin' me, 'till it's hurtin' me.

A#7 D#m
Ooh, baby love.

Outro

            C#
Don't throw our love away.

  F#   C#
‖: Don't throw our love away. :‖ *Repeat and fade*

Back in My Arms Again

Words and Music by Brian Holland,
Lamont Dozier and Edward Holland

Melody:

All day long I hear my tel-e-phone ring,

F/C C Dm/C F G Em Am

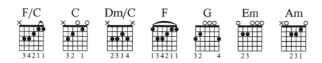

Intro   ‖: F/C | C | Dm/C | C   :‖

Verse 1

  C   F/C
All day long I hear my tele - phone ring,

          C   F/C
Friends calling, giving their advice.

           C   F/C
From the boy I love I should break away,

             C   F/C
'Cause heart - aches he'll bring one day.

F   G
I lost him once through friends advice,

     Em   Am
But it's not gonna happen twice.

F   G
'Cause all advice ever's gotten me

     Em   Am
Was many long and sleepless nights. ___ Ooh!

Chorus 1

F/C   C
But now he's back in my arms a - gain,

F/C   C
Right by my side.

F/C   C
I got him back in my arms a - gain,

F/C   C
So satis - fied. Ooh!

Verse 2

C   F/C
It's easy for friends to say let __ him go,

  C   F/C
But I'm the one who needs him so.

C   F/C
It's his love that makes ___ me strong;

     C   F/C
With - out him I can't go on.

F   G
This time I'll live my life at ease

     Em   Am
Being happy lovin' whom I please.

F   G
And each time we make romance

     Em   Am
I'll be thankful for a second chance. ___ Ooh!

Chorus 2

F/C   C
'Cause he's back in my arms a - gain,

F/C   C
Right by my side.

F/C   C
I've got him back in my arms a - gain,

F/C   C
So satis - fied. Ooh!

Verse 3

C   F/C
How can Mary tell me what ___ to do

    C   F/C
When she lost her love so true?

   C   F/C
And Flo, she don't know,

      C   F/C
'Cause the boy she loves is a Ro - meo.

F   G
 I listened once to my friends' advice,

    Em   Am
But it's not gonna happen twice.

F   G
 'Cause all advice ever's gotten me

    Em   Am
Was many long and sleepless nights. ___ Ooh!

Chorus 3

F/C   C
 I got him back in my arms a - gain,

F/C   C
 Right by my side.

F/C   C
 I got him back in my arms a - gain,

F/C   C
 So satis - fied. Ooh.

Outro

  F/C   C
‖: (Got him back in my arms a - gain,

F/C C
 Satis - fied.) :‖ *Repeat and fade w/ lead vocal ad lib.*

Ball of Confusion
(That's What the World Is Today)

Words and Music by
Norman Whitfield and Barrett Strong

C   F
1 3 3 3   1 3 4 2 1 1

Intro ‖: N.C.(C) | :‖ *Play 3 times*

Verse 1

C
People movin' out, people movin' in.

Because of the color of their skin.

Run, run, run, but you sure can't hide.

An eye for an eye, a tooth for a tooth.

Vote for me and I'll set you free.

Rap on, brother rap on!

Well, the only person talkin' 'bout, "Love thy brother," is the preacher.

And it seems nobody's intr'ested in learning but the teacher.

Segregation! Determination! Demonstration! Integration!

Aggravation! Humiliation! Obligation to our nation!

Chorus 1	C (Ball of confusion.) Oh yeah, that's what the world is today.
	(Mmm, hey, hey.)
Verse 2	C The sale of pills are at an all-time high.
	Young folks walkin' 'round with their head in the sky.
	Cities a-flame in the summertime. No, the beat goes on.
	Evolution! Revolution! Gun control! The sound of soul!
	Shooting rockets to the moon! Kids growin' up too soon!
	Politicians say, "More taxes will solve ev'rything."
	And the band played on.
	So, round and around and around we go.
	Where the world is headed said, "Nobody knows."
Bridge 1	| N.C.(C) | | (F) | | | (G) | | F Ah, Great Googa Mooga, can't you hear me talkin' to ya?

Chorus 2
       C
Just a ball of confusion. Oh yeah, that's what the world is today.

(Hey, hey, yeah.)

Verse 3
       C
Fear in the air, tension ev'rywhere.

Unemployment risin' fast, the Beatles' new record's a gas.

And the only safe place to live is on an Indian reservation.

And the band played on.

Eve of destruction! Tax deduction! City inspectors! Bill collectors!

Mod clothes in demand! Population out of hand!

Suicide! Too many bills! Yuppies movin' to the hills!

People all over the world they're shoutin', "End the war".

And the band played on.

Bridge 2
| N.C.(C) | | | (F) | | |
| (G) | | | |

    F
Great Googa Mooga, can't you hear me talkin' to ya?

Outro
       C
‖: Ball of confusion. That's what the world is today.

Yeah, yeah. :‖ *Repeat and fade w/ lead vocal ad lib.*

Bernadette

Words and Music by Brian Holland,
Lamont Dozier and Edward Holland

Melody:

Ber - na- dette,   peo-ple are search- in' for

Tune down 1/2 step:
(low to high) E♭ - A♭ - D♭ - G♭ - B♭ - E♭

E   D   C   B   Am   G

Em   Am7   D7sus4   G/B   D7

Intro | E | |

Chorus 1
E   D
Bernadette,   people are searchin' for

C   B   D
  The kind of love that we possess.

E   D
Some go on   searchin' their whole life through

C   Am   B   N.C.
  And never find the love I've found in you.

Verse 1
G   Em   Am7   D7sus4
  And when I speak of you, I see envy in other men's ___ eyes.

G   Em   Am7   D7sus4
  And I'm well aware of what's on their minds.

Am7   G/B   D7sus4   D7
  They pretend to be my friend when all the time

Am7   G/B   D7sus4   D7
  They long to ___ persuade you from ___ my side.

  Am7   G/B
They give the world and all ___ they own

  D7sus4   D7
For just one moment we have known.

Chorus 2

<pre>
E   D
Bernadette,   they want to because

C   B   D
  Of the pride that it gives.

     E   D   C
But Bernadette,   I want you because

Am   B   N.C.
I need you to live.
</pre>

Verse 2

<pre>
G   Em Am7   D7sus4
  But while I live only to hold ___ you

G   Em   Am7   D7sus4
  Some other men ___ they long to con - trol you.

Am7   G/B   D7sus4   D7
  But how can they control you, Bernadette,

    Am7   G/B   D7sus4   D7
When they cannot con - trol themselves, Bernadette,

    Am7   Bm
From wanting you, needing you,

D7sus4   D7   E
  But darlin'   you belong ___ to me.
</pre>

Bridge

<pre>
    D   C
I'll tell the world you belong ___ to me.

   B   D   E
I'll tell the world   you're the soul of me.

    D   C   Am   B
I'll tell the world you're a part of me,   Bernadette.

G   C   Em
In your arms I find the kind of peace of mind

                    B
The world is searching for.

    G   C
But you, you give me the joy this heart of mine

    Em   B
Has always been longing for.
</pre>

Verse 3

```
G        Em       Am7           D7sus4
   In you I have what other men long for.

G    Em                 Am7           D7sus4
   All men need someone to worship and a - dore.

Am7          G/B           D7sus4              D7
   That's why I treasure you and place you high above.

Am7          G/B      Am7      D7
   For the only joy in life    is to be loved.

Am7       Bm          D7sus4    D7          E
   So what - ever you do, Bernadette,     keep on lovin' me.

D                    C      Am      B           N.C.
Bernadette, keep on needing me.   Bernadette. (Ah.) Bernadette.
```

Outro

```
   E                    D
‖: Bernadette, you're the soul of me.

          C           B          D
More than a dream, you're a prayer to me.

      E                  D
And Bernadette, you mean more to me

          C       Am B          D
Than a wom - an was ever meant to be.    :‖ Repeat and fade
```

Being with You

Words and Music by
William "Smokey" Robinson

Melody:

I don't care what they think __ a-bout me, and __

(Capo 3rd fret)

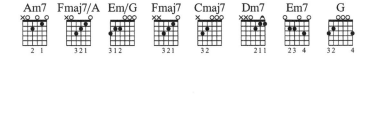

Am7   Fmaj7/A   Em/G   Fmaj7   Cmaj7   Dm7   Em7   G

Intro

|Am7 | |Fmaj7/A | |
|Am7 |Em/G |Fmaj7 | |

Chorus 1

Cmaj7   **Am7** **Dm7**
I don't care what they think ___ about ___ me and

Cmaj7   **Am7**
I don't care what they say.

Cmaj7   **Am7** **Dm7**
I don't care what they think ___ if you're ___ leaving,

Cmaj7   **Am7**
I'm gonna beg you to stay.

Cmaj7   **Am7** **Dm7**
I don't care if they start ___ to a - void me;

Cmaj7   **Am7**
I don't care what they do.

Cmaj7   **Am7** **Dm7**
I don't care about an - ything ___ else but

Cmaj7
Being with you, being with you.

Verse 1

Cmaj7   Am7 Cmaj7   Am7 Cmaj7
Honey, don't go,   don't leave this scene,

   Fmaj7   Dm7 Fmaj7   Dm7 Fmaj7
To be out of the picture, ___ and off of the screen.

Cmaj7   Am7 Cmaj7   Am7 Cmaj7
Don't let them say _____ we told you so,

   Fmaj7   Dm7 Fmaj7   Dm7 Fmaj7
They tell me you'll love me ___ and then let me go.

Em7   Am7
I've heard the warning voice from friends and my relations;

Fmaj7   G
They tell me all about your heartbreak reputation.

Chorus 2   *Repeat Chorus 1*

Sax Solo   *Repeat Intro*

Verse 2

Cmaj7   Am7   Cmaj7   Am7 Cmaj7
People can change,   they always do.

Fmaj7   Dm7 Fmaj7   Dm7 Fmaj7
Haven't they noticed ___ the changes in you?

Cmaj7 Am7   Cmaj7 Am7 Cmaj7
Or can it be that like love I am blind,

   Fmaj7   Dm7   Fmaj7 Dm7 Fmaj7
Do I want it so much 'till ___ it's all in my mind?

Em7   Am7
One thing I know for sure is really, really real,

Fmaj7   G
I never felt before the way you make me feel.

Chorus 3   *Repeat Chorus 1*

Outro

            Cmaj7 Am7
‖: Being with you,

            Cmaj7 Am7
Being with you.   :‖ *Repeat and fade*
                             w/ lead vocal ad lib.

Ben

Words by Don Black
Music by Walter Scharf

Melody:

Ben,   the two of us need look no more.

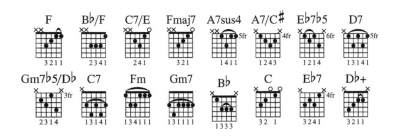

Intro ‖: F   B♭/F   │ F   B♭/F   :‖

Verse 1

F   C7/E
Ben, the two of us need look no more.

F   C7/E
We both found what we were looking for.

Fmaj7   A7sus4
With a friend to call my own,

　A7/C♯   E♭7♭5
I'll never be a - lone,

　　D7   Gm7♭5/D♭
And you my friend will see

　　C7   F   B♭/F   F B♭/F
You've got a friend in ___ me. (You've got a friend in me.)

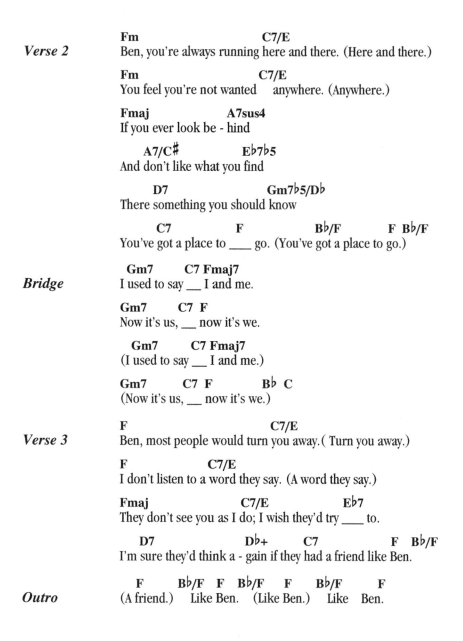

Verse 2

Fm   C7/E
Ben, you're always running here and there. (Here and there.)

Fm   C7/E
You feel you're not wanted   anywhere. (Anywhere.)

Fmaj   A7sus4
If you ever look be - hind

   A7/C♯   E♭7♭5
And don't like what you find

    D7   Gm7♭5/D♭
There something you should know

    C7   F   B♭/F   F B♭/F
You've got a place to ___ go. (You've got a place to go.)

Bridge

  Gm7   C7 Fmaj7
I used to say ___ I and me.

Gm7   C7 F
Now it's us, ___ now it's we.

  Gm7   C7 Fmaj7
(I used to say ___ I and me.)

Gm7   C7 F   B♭ C
(Now it's us, ___ now it's we.)

Verse 3

F   C7/E
Ben, most people would turn you away.(Turn you away.)

F   C7/E
I don't listen to a word they say. (A word they say.)

Fmaj   C7/E   E♭7
They don't see you as I do; I wish they'd try ___ to.

  D7   D♭+   C   F B♭/F
I'm sure they'd think a - gain if they had a friend like Ben.

Outro

   F   B♭/F F B♭/F   F   B♭/F   F
(A friend.)   Like Ben. (Like Ben.)   Like   Ben.

Dancing in the Street

Words and Music by Marvin Gaye,
Ivy Hunter and William Stevenson

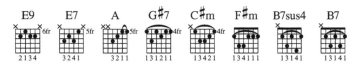

E9	E7	A	G#7	C#m	F#m	B7sus4	B7
6fr	5fr	5fr	4fr	4fr			
2 1 3 4	3 2 4 1	3 2 1 1	1 3 1 2 1 1	1 3 4 2 1	1 3 4 1 1 1	1 3 1 4 1	1 3 1 4 1

Intro ‖: E9 E7 | E9 E7 :‖

Verse 1

    E9   E7   E9   E7
Call - ing out ___ around ___ the world,

       E9   E7   E9 E7
Are you ready for a brand new beat?

E9   E7   E9   E7
Summers here ___ and the time is right

    E9   E7   E9
For dancing in the street.

          E7   E9   E7   E9 E7
They're danc - ing in Chica - go, (Dancing in the street.)

       E9   E7   E9
Down in New Orleans, (Dancing in the street.)

   E7   E9   E7
In New York Cit - y. (Dancing in the street.)

    E9   E7   A
All ___ we need ___ is mu - sic, sweet music.

There'll be music everywhere.

       E9   E7   E9   E7
There'll be swinging, sway - ing and records play - ing,

E9   E7   E9 E7
Dancing in the street, ___ oh.

Chorus 1

G#7

It doesn't matter what you wear, just as long as you are there.

         C#m

F#m

So come on, ev'ry guy grab a girl.

B7sus4   B7

Ev'rywhere around ___ the world,

        E9   E7

They'll be dancing. (Dancing in the street.)

E9   E7   E9   E7   E9

They're dancing in the street. ___ (Dancing in the street.)

Verse 2

E7   E9 E7   E9   E7

This is an invita - tion a - cross the na - tion,

E9   E7   E9

A chance for folks to meet.

E7   E9   E7   E9   E7

There'll be laughing, sing - ing and music swing - ing,

E9   E7   E9

Dancing in the street.

     E7   E9   E7

Phila - delphia, P.A., ___ (Dancing in the street.)

E9   E7   E9   E7

Balti - more and D.C., ___ now. (Dancing in the street.)

E9   E7   E9   E7

Can't forget the Motor Cit - y. (Dancing in the street.)

     E9   E7   A

All ___ we need ___ is mu - sic, sweet music.

There'll be music everywhere.

     E9   E7   E9   E7

There'll be swinging, sway - ing and records play - ing,

E9   E7   E9 E7

Dancing in the street, ___ oh.

Chorus 2

G#7   **C#m**
It doesn't matter what you wear, just as long as you are there.

F#m
So come on, ev'ry guy grab a girl.

B7sus4   **B7**   **E9**   **E7**
Ev'rywhere around ___ the world, they're danc - ing,

E9   **E7**   **E9**   **E7**
They're dancing in the street. ___ (Dancing in the street.)

E9   **E7** **E9** **E7**   **E9**
Outro   Way down in L.A., ___ every day,

                   E7   **E9**   **E7**
They're dancing in the street. ___ (Dancing in the street.)

E9   **E7**   **E9** **E7**   **E9**
Let's form a big strong line, ___ get in time,

                   E7   **E9**   **E7**
We're dancing in the street. ___ (Dancing in the street.)

E9   **E7**   **E9** **E7**   **E9**
Across the ocean blue, ___ me and you,

                   E7   **E9**   **E7**
We're dancing in the street. ___ (Dancing in the street.) *Fade out*

Easy

Words and Music by
Lionel Richie

Know it sounds fun-ny, but I just can't stand the pain. _

(Capo 1st fret)

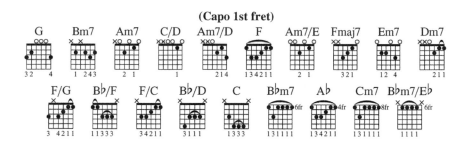

G	Bm7	Am7	C/D	Am7/D	F	Am7/E	Fmaj7	Em7	Dm7
F/G	Bb/F	F/C	Bb/D	C	Bbm7	Ab	Cm7	Bbm7/Eb	

Intro |G   Bm7 |Am7   C/D |G   Bm7 |Am7 |

Verse 1
```
        G                    Bm7               Am7           C/D
        Know it sounds funny, but I just can't stand the pain.

        G           Bm 7              Am7    Am7/D G
        Girl, I'm leav - ing you tomorrow.

                    Bm7                           Am7        C/D
        Seems to me, ___ girl, you know I've done all ___ I can.

        G           Bm7               Am7           C/D
        You see, I begged, stole and I bor - rowed. Yeah,    ooh.
```

Chorus 1
```
                        G        Bm7 Am7
        That's why I'm eas - y, (Ah.)

            Am7/D           G           Bm7 Am7   C/D
        I'm easy like Sunday morn - ing. (Ah.)

                        G        Bm7 Am7
        That's why I'm eas - y, (Ah.)

            Am7/D               F Am7/E  C/D G
        I'm easy like Sunday morn        -      ing.
```

Verse 2

G   Bm7   Am7   C/D
Why in the world ___ would anybody put chains ___ on me?

G   Bm7   Am7   Am7/D   G
I've paid ___ my dues to make it.

               Bm7   Am7   Am7/D
Ev'rybody wants ___ me to be what they want ___ me to be.

G   Bm7   Am7   Am7/D
I'm not hap - py when I try to fake ___ it, no.

Chorus 2

                    G   Bm7   Am7
Ooh, that's why I'm eas - y, (Ah.)

Am7/D   G   Bm7   Am7   C/D
I'm easy like Sunday morn - ing. (Ah.)

            G   Bm7   Am7
That's why I'm eas - y, (Ah.)

Am7/D   F   Am7/E   C/D   G
I'm easy like Sunday morn   -   ing.

Bridge

        Fmaj7   Em7   Dm7   F/G
I wanna be high,   so   high.

        Am7   Fmaj7   Em7   Dm7   F/G
I wan - na be free to know the things I do are   right.

       Am7   Fmaj7   Am7   Dm7   F/G   Bb/F   F/C   Bb/D   C
I wan - na be free,   just   me,   oh, babe.

Guitar Solo | G   Bm7 | Am7 C/D | G   Bm7 | Am7 Am7/D |
                      | G   Bm7 | Am7 C/D | G   Bm7 | Am7 |

Chorus 3
```
Am7                    G        Bm7 Am7
  That's why I'm eas - y, (Ah.)
```

```
    Am7/D                 G          Bm7  Am7  C/D
I'm easy like Sunday morn - ing. (Ah.)
```

```
                   G        Bm7 Am7
That's why I'm eas - y, (Ah.)
```

```
    Am7/D               G        Bm7     Am7  Bbm7
I'm easy like Sunday morn - ing. (Ah.)    Whoa.
```

Chorus 4
```
            Ab        Cm7 Bbm7
'Cause I'm eas - y, (Ah.)
```

```
Bbm7/Eb              Ab        Cm7  Bbm7  Bbm7/Eb
Easy like Sunday morn - ing. (Ah.)
```

```
            Ab        Cm7 Bbm7
'Cause I'm eas - y, (Ah.)
```

```
    Bbm7/Eb              Ab          Cm7  Bbm7
I'm easy like Sunday morn - ing. (Ah.)          *Fade out*
```

For Once in My Life

Melody:

Words by Ronald Miller
Music by Orlando Murden

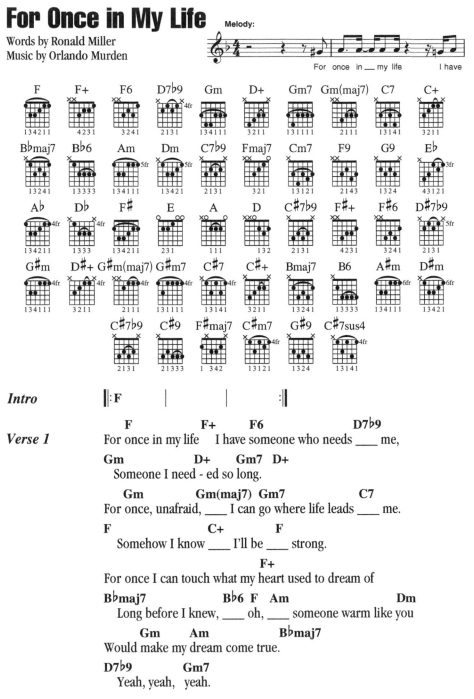

For once in __ my life   I have

Intro   ‖: F | | | :‖

Verse 1

      F   F+   F6   D7♭9

For once in my life   I have someone who needs ____ me,

Gm   **D+**   **Gm7** **D+**

Someone I need - ed so long.

       Gm   **Gm(maj7) Gm7**   **C7**

For once, unafraid, ____ I can go where life leads ____ me.

F   **C+**   **F**

Somehow I know ____ I'll be ____ strong.

                            F+

For once I can touch what my heart used to dream of

B♭maj7   **B♭6 F Am**   **Dm**

Long before I knew, ____ oh, ____ someone warm like you

      Gm   **Am**   **B♭maj7**

Would make my dream come true.

D7♭9   **Gm7**

Yeah, yeah, yeah.

Verse 2

C7♭9 Fmaj7 F+ F6   D7♭9
For once my life I won't let sorrow ____ hurt me,

Gm   C7
 Not like it's hurt me before. ____ (Not like it's hurt before.)

     Gm   Gm(maj7)   Gm7   C7
For once ____ I have something I know ____ won't desert ____ me.

Fmaj7   F   Cm7
 I'm not a - lone anymore. (I'm not alone anymore.)

F9 F   F+
 For once I can say this is mine, you can't take it.

   B♭maj7   G9
Long as I know I have love ____ I can make it.

   F   Dm   Gm   C7
For once in my life I have ____ someone who ____ needs me.

Interlude

 N.C. (F) (E♭) (A♭) (D♭) (C7♭9)
 (Someone ____ who needs me.

 (F♯)   (E)   (A) (D) (C♯7♭9)
 Someone ____ who needs me.)

Harmonica Solo |F# F#+ |F#6 D#7b9 |G#m D#+ |G#m D#+ |

(For once in my

|G#m G#m(maj7) |G#m7 C#7 |F# C#+ |F# |

Life.)

| |F#+ | Bmaj7 | B6 |A#m |

|D#m |G#m A#m | Bmaj7 D#7b9 G#m7

(Make my dreams come true.)

Verse 3

C#7b9 F#   F#+   F#6   D#7b9
For   once in my life, ___ I won't ___ let sorrow hurt me,

G#m   C#9
   Not like it's hurt me before. ___ (Not like it's hurt before.)

   G#m   G#m(maj7) G#m7   C#7
For once I have some - thing I know ___ won't desert ___ me.

F#maj7   F#6   C#m7
   I'm not alone ___ any - more. (I'm not alone anymore.)

   F#   F#+
For once I can say this is   mine, you can't take it.

Bmaj7   G#9
   Long as I know I have love ___ I can make it.

   F#   D#m   G#m7   C#7sus4
For once in my life, I have   someone who needs me.

Outro

   N.C. (F#)   (E) (A)   (D) (C#7b9)
|| : Someone who   needs me.   : || *Repeat and fade*
                                              w/ lead vocal ad lib.

Get Ready

Words and Music by
William "Smokey" Robinson

Melody:

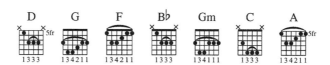

I nev-er met a girl who makes _ me feel _ the way that

Intro

| N.C.(D) | | | D | | G F |
| D | | G F |

Verse 1

   D   G F   D
I never met a girl who makes me feel the way that you do,

       G F
You're all right.

     D   G F   D
When - ever I'm asked who makes my dreams real, I say that you do

       G F
You're out of sight.

   D   G F
So, fe, fi, fo, fum

  D   G F
Lookout baby, 'cause here I come.

Chrous 1

F   Bb
And I'm bringing you a love that's true.

  Gm C
So get ready, so get ready.

F   Bb
I'm gonna try makin' love to you.

  Gm C   D
So get ready, so get ready, here I come.

       G F D
(Get ready, 'cause here I come.) I'm on ___ my way.

      G F
(Get ready, 'cause here I come.)

Verse 2

  D   G F D
If you wanna play hide and seek with love, let me re - mind you,

  G F
It's alright.

  D   G F D
A lovin', you're gonna miss in the time it takes to find you.

  G F
It's outta sight.

  D   G F
So, fiddle dee, dee, fiddle dee, dum

D   G F
Lookout, baby, 'cause here I come.

Chorus 2   *Repeat Chorus 1*

Sax Solo |D | G F |D | G F |
        |G A |G A |G A G |Bb A G |

Verse 3

D   G F   D
All my friends should want you too I'll under - stand it.

            G F
Be alright.

D   G F   D
I hope I get to you before they do, the way I planned it

              G F
Be outta sight.

D   G F
So, tweedle, dee, dee, tweedle dee, dum

D   G   F
Look out baby 'cause here I come.

Chorus 3

F   Bb
  And I'm bringing you a love that's true.

     Gm   C
So get ready, so get ready.

F   Bb
  I'm gonna try makin' love to you.

     Gm   C   D
So get ready, so get ready, here I come.

                                    G   F   D
(Get ready, 'cause here I come.) I'm on ____ my way.

                            G F
(Get ready, 'cause here I come.)

D   G F
(Get ready 'cause here I come.) *Fade out*

Got to Be There

Words and Music by
Elliott Willensky

Melody:

Got to be there, got to be there

(Capo 1st fret)

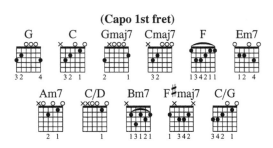

G C Gmaj7 Cmaj7 F Em7

Am7 C/D Bm7 F#maj7 C/G

Intro |G |C |G |C |

Verse 1

G   Gmaj7   Cmaj7   C
Got to be there, got to be there in the morn - ing

        F   Em7
When she says hello to the world.

G   Gmaj7   Cmaj7   C
Got to be there, got to be there, bring her good   times

        F   Em7
And show her that she's my girl.

Am7   C/D   Gmaj7
Oh,   what a feeling there'll be

        C/D   Gmaj7 Bm7 Em7
The moment I know she loves   me.

                C/D
'Cause when I look in her eyes I realize

                             F#maj7 C/D
I need her sharing the world be - side   me.

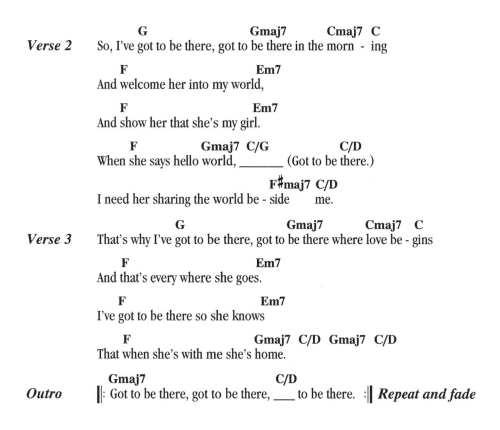

Verse 2

          G   **Gmaj7**   **Cmaj7** **C**
So, I've got to be there, got to be there in the morn - ing

         F   **Em7**
And welcome her into my world,

         F   **Em7**
And show her that she's my girl.

          F   **Gmaj7** **C/G**   **C/D**
When she says hello world, _____ (Got to be there.)

                                  F#maj7 **C/D**
I need her sharing the world be - side   me.

Verse 3

               G   **Gmaj7**   **Cmaj7** **C**
That's why I've got to be there, got to be there where love be - gins

         F   **Em7**
And that's every where she goes.

         F   **Em7**
I've got to be there so she knows

         F   **Gmaj7** **C/D** **Gmaj7** **C/D**
That when she's with me she's home.

Outro

   Gmaj7   **C/D**
‖: Got to be there, got to be there, ___ to be there. :‖ *Repeat and fade*

Heatwave
(Love Is Like a Heatwave)

Words and Music by Edward Holland,
Lamont Dozier and Brian Holland

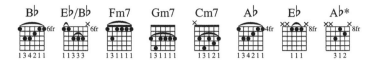

Bb Eb/Bb Fm7 Gm7 Cm7 Ab Eb Ab*

Intro

```
||: Bb  Eb/Bb  Bb  Eb/Bb :||  Play 3 times
| Bb  N.C.  | Fm7      | Gm7      | Cm7          |
|           | Fm7      | Gm7      | Cm7          |
|           | Fm7      | Gm7      | Ab           |
| Bb        | Eb Ab* Eb Ab* | Eb Ab* Eb Ab* | Eb Ab* Eb Ab* |
```

Verse 1

Eb N.C.   Fm7
    Whenever I'm with him,

Gm7   Cm7   Fm7
    Something in - side starts to burnin'.

Gm7   Cm7
    And I'm filled with desire.

Fm7   Gm7
    Could it be a devil in me,

   Ab   Bb
Or is this the way love's sup - posed to be?

Chorus 1

      Eb   Ab*   Eb Ab*
It's like a heat - wave

Eb Ab*   Eb Ab* Eb Ab* Eb Ab*
    Burn - in' in my heart.

Eb Ab* Eb   Ab* Eb Ab* Eb Ab*
    I can't keep from cry - in',

Eb   Ab*   Eb Ab*   Eb Ab* Eb Ab*
    It's tearing me a - part.

Verse 2

Eb N.C.   Fm7
    Whenever he calls my name,

Gm7 Cm7
    Soft, low, sweet and plain,

  Fm7   Gm7
I feel, yeah, yeah,

  Cm7
I feel that burnin' flame.

   Fm7   Gm7
Has high blood pressure got a hold on me,

    Ab   Bb
Or is this the way love's sup - posed to be?

Chorus 2   *Repeat Chorus 1*

Interlude

Eb N.C.	Fm7	Gm7	Cm7		

                 (Ooh, _____   ooh, ___ heatwave.)

Fm7	Gm7	Cm7		

   (Ooh, _____   ooh, ___ heatwave.)

Fm7	Gm7	Ab	Bb	

Verse 3

Eb N.C.   Fm7
    Sometimes I stare in space,

Gm7   Cm7
    Tears all over my face.

    Fm7   Gm7
I can't ex - plain it, don't under - stand it,

    Cm7
I ain't never felt like this before.

    Fm7   Gm7
Now that funny feelin' has me amazed.

    Ab   Bb
I don't know what to do, my head's in a haze.

      Eb
It's like a heatwave.

| | N.C.   Fm7   Gm7 |
| *Verse 4* | Yeah, yeah, yeah, yeah. (Well, it's al - right, girl.) |

       Cm7
Whoa, ho. (Go ahead, girl.)

       Fm7   **Gm7 Cm7**
Yeah, yeah, yeah, yeah, ho. (Ain't nothin' but a song, girl.)

Fm7   **Gm7**
  Don't pass up this chance.

A♭   **B♭**
  It's time for a new romance.

E♭
Heatwave.

| | N.C.   **Fm7**   **Gm7 Cm7** |
| *Outro* | Yeah, yeah, yeah, yeah, ho. |

                    Fm7
Yeah, don't you know it's like a heatwave.

Gm7   **Cm7**
Burnin' right here in my heart.

     Fm7   **Gm7 Cm7**
Yeah, yeah, yeah, yeah, ho.   *Fade out*

I Can't Get Next to You

Words and Music by
Barrett Strong and Norman Whitfield

I can make your grey sky blue. ____

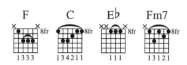

Intro

| F | C | |

Verse 1

    C Eb   C
I can turn your gray sky blue.

               Eb   C
I can make it rain   when - ever I want it to.

             Eb   C
I can build a castle from a single grain of sand.

                  Eb   C
I can make the ship sail ____ huh, on dry land.

F   Fm7   C
  But my life is incom - plete and I'm so blue,

       F   Fm7   C N.C.
'Cause I can't ____ get next to you.

Chorus 1

   N.C.(C)   (G) (Bb) (C)   (Eb) (C)
(I can't get next to _____ you, babe.)

                        (F) (Eb) (C)
Next to you, (I can't get next to) I just can't.

        (G) (Bb) (C)   (Eb) (C)
(I can't get next to ____ you, babe.)

            (F) (Eb) (C)
(I can't get next to you.)

Verse 2

```
        C       Eb    C
I can fly like a bird in the sky,
```

```
                    Eb         C
And I can buy any - thing that money can buy.
```

```
                        Eb  C
(Oh, I) can turn a river      into a raging fire.
```

```
                    Eb  C
I can live forever       if I so desire.
```

```
F             Fm7        C
  I don't want ____ it, all ____ these things I can do,
```

```
F          Fm7
  'Cause I ____ can't get next to
```

Chorus 2

```
N.C.(C)             (G)  (Bb)  (C)        (Eb)   (C)
You.(I can't get next to _____ you,...) No matter what I do.
```

```
                      (F)  (Eb)  (C)  (Bb)  (C)
(I can't get next to you.)          Ah, ____ ya.
```

Interlude

```
| N.C.(Drums) |              | C            |                      |
|             |              |              |          | Eb  C  Eb |
| C N.C.        Eb  C  Eb | C N.C.          |
```

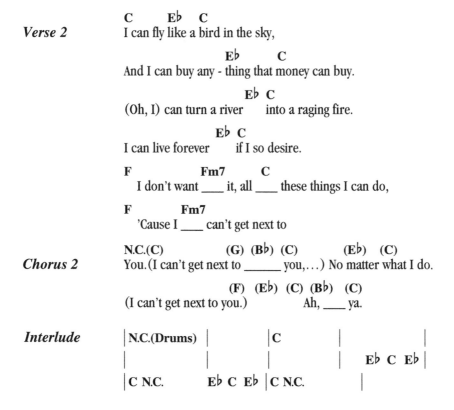

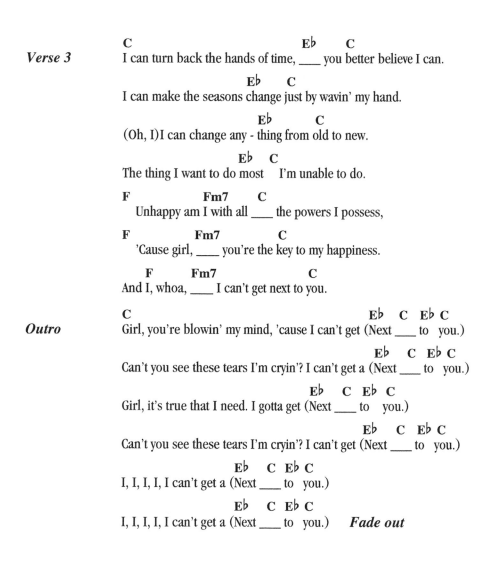

Verse 3

    C   Eb   C
I can turn back the hands of time, ___ you better believe I can.

                      Eb   C
I can make the seasons change just by wavin' my hand.

                     Eb   C
(Oh, I)I can change any - thing from old to new.

                       Eb   C
The thing I want to do most   I'm unable to do.

F   Fm7   C
  Unhappy am I with all ___ the powers I possess,

F   Fm7   C
  'Cause girl, ___ you're the key to my happiness.

    F   Fm7   C
And I, whoa, ___ I can't get next to you.

Outro

  C   Eb   C Eb C
Girl, you're blowin' my mind, 'cause I can't get (Next ___ to you.)

                                                Eb   C Eb C
Can't you see these tears I'm cryin'? I can't get a (Next ___ to you.)

                                 Eb   C Eb C
Girl, it's true that I need. I gotta get (Next ___ to you.)

                                            Eb   C Eb C
Can't you see these tears I'm cryin'? I can't get (Next ___ to you.)

                     Eb   C Eb C
I, I, I, I, I can't get a (Next ___ to you.)

                     Eb   C Eb C
I, I, I, I, I can't get a (Next ___ to you.)   ***Fade out***

How Sweet It Is
(To Be Loved by You)

Words and Music by Edward Holland,
Lamont Dozier and Brian Holland

Melody:

How sweet it   is ___   to   be ___ loved   by

F   Dm7   C   Am   G

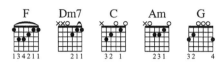

134211   211   32 1   231   32   4

Chorus 1

    F   Dm7   C
How sweet it is ___ to be loved by you. Yes, baby, ooh.

    F   Dm7   C   F
How sweet it is ___ to be loved by you. Ooh, ba - by.

Verse 1

   C   Am
I needed the shelter   of someone's arms,

   G   F
And there you ___ were.

    C   Am
I needed someone to understand my ups and downs,

   G   F
And there you ___ were.

   C   F
With sweet love and devotion,

   C   F
Deeply touching my ___ emotions.

         C   F
I wanna stop and thank you, baby.

             C   F
I wanna stop ___ and thank you baby. Yeah, now.

Chorus 2

    F   Dm7   C
How sweet it is ___ to be loved by you. Oh, baby.

    F   Dm7   C   F
How sweet it is ___ to be loved by you. Yes, it is.

Verse 2

C   Am
Close my eyes at night,

G   F
And wonder what would I be with - out you in my life.

C   Am
Ev'rything was just a bore.

G   F
All the things I did, seems I've done 'em before.

C   F
But you brighten up all my days

C   F
With a love so sweet in so many ways.

       C   F
I wanna stop ___ and thank you, baby.

     C   F
I wanna ___ stop and thank you, baby. Yeah.

Chorus 3

F   Dm7   C
How sweet it is ___ to be loved by you. Oh, yes it is, baby.

F   Dm7   C   F
How sweet it is ___ to be loved by you. Yes, it is, ba - by.

Instrumental | C | Am | G | F |

Verse 3

C   F
You were better to me that I've been to myself,

C   F
For me there's you and nobody else.

C   F
Stop and thank you baby.

      C   F
I want to stop ___ and thank you baby, oh.

Chorus 3

F   Dm7   C
How sweet it is ___ to be loved by you. Tell the truth, baby.

F   Dm7   C
How sweet it is ___ to be loved by you.

Well it's like sugar to my soul.

F   Dm7   C
How sweet it is ___ to be loved by you.

Oh, yes it is, baby. ***Fade out***

I Can't Help Myself
(Sugar Pie, Honey Bunch)

Words and Music by Brian Holland,
Lamont Dozier and Edward Holland

Melody:

Su - gar pie, hon - ey bunch,

C   G   Dm   C/E   F   C6

Intro

| N.C.(C) | | | |
| | | | |

Verse 1

  C   G
Sugar pie, honey bunch, you know that I ___ love you.

        Dm   C/E F   G C6
I can't help myself, I love you and nobody else.

  C   G
In and out my life, you come and you go,

        Dm
Leaving just your picture behind.

              C/E F   G C6
And I kissed it a   thousand times.

Verse 2

          C
When you snap your finger or wink your eyes,

        G
I come a runnin' to you.

          Dm
I'm tied to your apron string,

              C/E   F   G   C6
And there's nothing ___ that I can do.   Oo.

Sax Solo

| C | | G | |
| Dm | G | F | G   C6 |

    Can't help myself, no, I can't help myself.

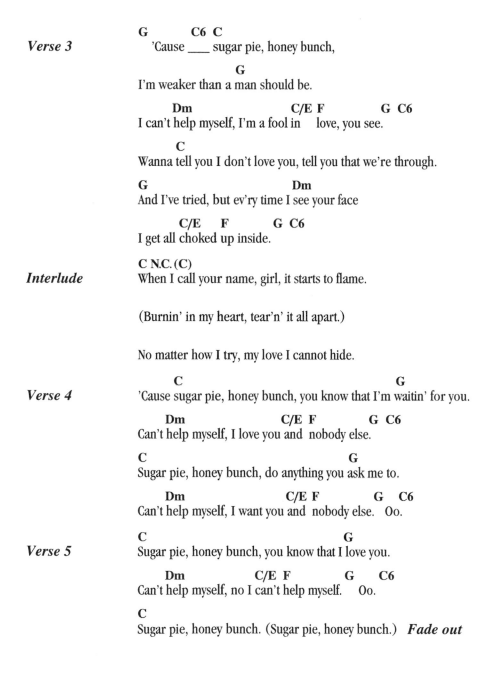

Verse 3

```
     G        C6  C
      'Cause ___ sugar pie, honey bunch,

                 G
I'm weaker than a man should be.

       Dm                  C/E F          G  C6
I can't help myself, I'm a fool in   love, you see.

       C
Wanna tell you I don't love you, tell you that we're through.

G                        Dm
And I've tried, but ev'ry time I see your face

       C/E     F          G  C6
I get all choked up inside.
```

Interlude

```
C N.C. (C)
When I call your name, girl, it starts to flame.


(Burnin' in my heart, tear'n' it all apart.)


No matter how I try, my love I cannot hide.
```

Verse 4

```
       C                                 G
'Cause sugar pie, honey bunch, you know that I'm waitin' for you.

       Dm                  C/E F          G  C6
Can't help myself, I love you and  nobody else.

C                        G
Sugar pie, honey bunch, do anything you ask me to.

       Dm                  C/E F          G  C6
Can't help myself, I want you and  nobody else.  Oo.
```

Verse 5

```
C                              G
Sugar pie, honey bunch, you know that I love you.

       Dm             C/E F         G    C6
Can't help myself, no I can't help myself.   Oo.

C
Sugar pie, honey bunch. (Sugar pie, honey bunch.)  *Fade out*
```

I Heard It Through the Grapevine

Words and Music by
Norman J. Whitfield
and Barrett Strong

Melody:

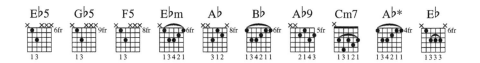

Oo, ___ I bet you won-dered how I knew

Eb5	Gb5	F5	Ebm	Ab	Bb	Ab9	Cm7	Ab*	Eb

Intro

‖: Eb5   Gb5 Eb5 | Gb5 F5 Eb5 :‖

| Eb5   Gb5 Eb5 | Gb5 F5 Ebm |

| Ab Ebm | Ab   Ebm |

| Ab Ebm | |

Verse 1

    Ab Ebm   Ab Ebm
Oo, ___ I bet you wondered how I knew

Ab Ebm Bb   Ab9
'Bout your plans to make me blue

    Ebm Ab   Ebm
With some other guy you knew be - fore.

    Ab Ebm Bb   Ab9
Between the two of us guys, you know I love you more.

    Cm7   Ab*   Eb   Ab*
It took me by surprise I must say when I found out yester - day.

Chorus 1

                       Eb   Ab* Eb
Don't you know that I heard it through the grape - vine.

      Ab*
Not much longer would you be mine.

          Eb   Ab* Eb
Oh, I heard it through the grape - vine.

      Ab*
Oh, I'm just about to lose my mind.

N.C.   Eb5   Gb5
Honey, honey, well. (Hear it through the grapevine,

Eb5   Gb5 F5 Eb5 Gb5 Eb5
Not much longer would you be   my baby.

Do, do…)

Verse 2

Gb5 F5   Ebm   Ab   Ebm
I   know a man ain't sup - posed to cry,

Ab Ebm Bb   Ab9
But these tears, I can't hold in - side.

      Ebm   Ab   Ebm
Losing you would end my life, you see.

Ab   Ebm Bb   Ab9
'Cause you   mean that much to me.

            Cm7   Ab*   Eb   Ab*
You could've told me your - self that you love someone else.

Chorus 2

        Eb   Ab*   Eb
Instead I heard it through the grape - vine.

      Ab*
Not much longer would you be mine.

      Eb   Ab*   Eb
Oh, I heard it through the grape - vine,

       Ab*
And I'm just about to lose my mind.

N.C.   Eb5   Gb5
Honey, honey, well. (Hear it through the grapevine,

Eb5   Gb5 F5 Eb5 Gb5 Eb5
Not much longer would you be   my baby.

      Gb5 F5
Do, do, do,   do, do.

Interlude | E♭m   A♭ E♭m | A♭ | E♭m   A♭ E♭m |

Verse 3
N.C.   E♭m   A♭   E♭m
People say believe half of what you see.

A♭   E♭m B♭   A♭9
Some and   none of what you hear.

               E♭m   A♭   E♭m
But I can't help from being con - fused.

A♭ E♭m B♭   A♭9
If   it's   true, please tell me dear.

               Cm7   A♭*   E♭   A♭*
Do you plan to let me go for the other guy you loved before?

                              E♭   A♭*   E♭
Chorus 3   Don't you know I heard it through the grape - vine.

               A♭*
Not much longer would you be mine.

               E♭   A♭*   E♭
Baby, I heard it through the grape - vine,

               A♭*
Ooh, I'm just about to lose my mind.

N.C.   E♭5   G♭5
Honey, honey, yeah. (Heard it through the grapevine,

E♭5   G♭5 F5 E♭5   G♭5 E♭5
Not much longer would you be   my baby.

Yeah, yeah…)

               G♭5 F5 E♭5 G♭5 E♭5   G♭5 F5   E♭5 G♭5 E♭5
Outro   Honey, hon - ey I know   that you're let - tin' me go.

G♭5 F5 E♭5   G♭5   E♭5
Said   I   heard it through the grape - vine.

     G♭5 F5 E♭5   G♭5   E5
Oo, _____ heard it through the grape - vine.   *Fade out*

I Want You Back

Words and Music by Freddie Perren,
Alphonso Mizell, Berry Gordy
and Deke Richards

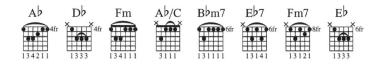

Intro ‖: A♭ |D♭ |Fm A♭/C D♭ A♭ |B♭m7 E♭7 A♭ :‖

A♭ D♭ E♭7 Fm A♭/C D♭ A♭ B♭m7 E♭7 A♭
Oh, ___ let me tell ya, now. Ooh, oo. (Mm, mm, mm.)

Verse 1
A♭ D♭
When I had you to myself, I didn't want you around.

Fm A♭/C D♭ A♭ B♭m7 E♭7 A♭
Those pretty fac - es al - ways made ___ you stand out in a crowd.

D♭
But someone picked you from the bunch, one glance was all it took.

Fm A♭/C D♭ A♭ B♭m7 E♭7 A♭
Now it's much too late ___ for me ___ to take a second look.

Chorus 1
A♭ D♭
Oh, baby, give me one more chance ___ (To show you that I love ya.)

Fm A♭/C D♭ A♭ B♭m7 E♭7 A♭
Won't you please let me _____ back in your heart.

D♭ B♭m7 E♭
Oh, darling, I was blind to let you go, (Let you go, baby.)

Fm A♭/C D♭ A♭ B♭m7 E♭7 A♭
But now since I see you in his arms (I want you back.)

Oh, I do now. (I want you back.) Ooh, ooh, baby. (I want you back.)

Yeah, yeah, yeah, yeah, (I want you back.) Yeah, now, now, now.

Verse 2

A♭   D♭
Trying to live without your love is one long sleepless night.

Fm   A♭/C   D♭ A♭ B♭m7 E♭7   A♭
Let me show ____ you, girl,   that I know wrong from right.

                                    D♭
Every street you walk on, I leave tear stains on the ground,

Fm   A♭/C   D♭   A♭ B♭m7 E♭7   A♭
Follow - ing the girl ____ I did - n't even   want a - round.

Let me tell you now.

A♭   D♭
Oh, baby, all I need is one ____ more chance

Chorus 2

(To show you that I love you.)

Fm   A♭/C D♭   A♭ B♭m7 E♭7 A♭
Won't you   please let   me _____ back in your heart.

                                    D♭   B♭m7   E♭
Oh, darling, I was blind to let you go. (Let you go, baby.)

      Fm A♭/C D♭ A♭
But now since I   see you

Interlude

Fm7 E♭   D♭   Fm7   E♭ D♭ A♭
In his arms,   uh, huh.

|Fm7 E♭ D♭ Fm7 | E♭   D♭   A♭ |
                    A buh, buh, buh, buh.

Fm7   E♭ D♭   A♭
 A buh, buh, buh, buh.

  Fm7   E♭ D♭   A♭
All I want a buh, buh, buh, buh.

  Fm7   E♭ D♭   A♭
All I need a buh, buh, buh, buh.

  Fm7   E♭ D♭   A♭
All I want a buh, buh, buh, buh.

  A♭   D♭
Verse 3   All I need, oh, just one more chance to show you that I love you.

Fm7 A♭/C D♭   A♭ B♭m7 E♭7 A♭
Baby, baby, baby, baby, baby,   baby.   (I want you back.)

Forget what happened then. Let me live again.

          D♭
Oh, baby I was blind to let you go,

  Fm A♭/C D♭ A♭ B♭m7 E♭7   A♭
But now since I   see you   in his arms ___ (I want you back.)

Spare me of this cost, give that girl love.

              D♭
Oh, baby, I need one more chance I tell you that I love you.

Fm A♭/C D♭   A♭ B♭m7 E♭7
Baby, ah,   baby, ah ba-by   ah.

A♭
 I want you back.   *Repeat and fade*

I Second That Emotion

Words and Music by
William "Smokey" Robinson
and Alfred Cleveland

May - be you wan-na give _ me kiss-es sweet, _____

A   G   D

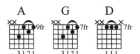

Intro |A   G | |D | |

Verse 1
D
Maybe you wanna give me kisses sweet,

But only for one night with no repeat.

And maybe you'll go away and never call.

             G   A   D
And a taste of honey's worse ___ than none at all.

Bridge 1
D   G   D
   Oh, little girl, in that case I don't want no part.
             G   D
I do believe that that would only break my heart.

Chorus 1
             D   A   G
Oh, but if you feel like lovin' me, if you got the no - tion,
             D
I second that e - motion.

                              A   G
Said, if you've feel like givin' me a lifetime of devo - tion,
             D   A   G
I second that e - motion.   Oh.

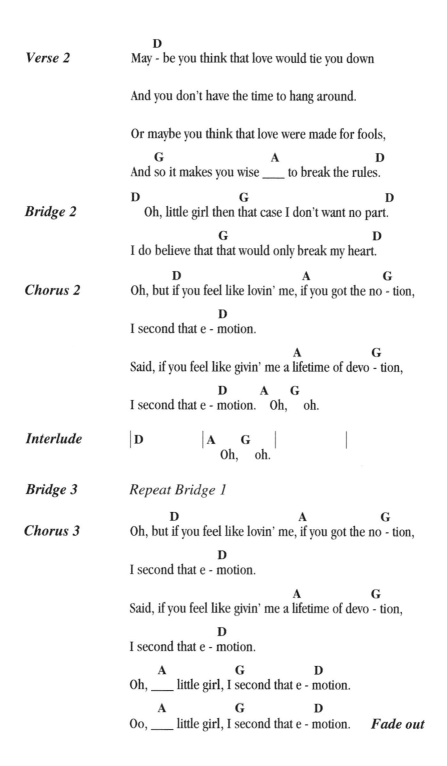

Verse 2
D
May - be you think that love would tie you down

And you don't have the time to hang around.

Or maybe you think that love were made for fools,

G   A   D
And so it makes you wise ___ to break the rules.

Bridge 2
D   G   D
  Oh, little girl then that case I don't want no part.

G   D
I do believe that that would only break my heart.

Chorus 2
D   A   G
Oh, but if you feel like lovin' me, if you got the no - tion,

D
I second that e - motion.

A   G
Said, if you feel like givin' me a lifetime of devo - tion,

D   A   G
I second that e - motion.   Oh,   oh.

Interlude
| D | A   G | |
            Oh,   oh.

Bridge 3
Repeat Bridge 1

Chorus 3
D   A   G
Oh, but if you feel like lovin' me, if you got the no - tion,

D
I second that e - motion.

A   G
Said, if you feel like givin' me a lifetime of devo - tion,

D
I second that e - motion.

A   G   D
Oh, ___ little girl, I second that e - motion.

A   G   D
Oo, ___ little girl, I second that e - motion.   *Fade out*

I Wish

Words and Music by
Stevie Wonder

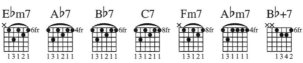

Look-ing back on when I ___ was a lit - tle nap - py head -

Ebm7   Ab7   Bb7   C7   Fm7   Abm7   Bb+7

Intro | N.C.(Ebm7) (Ab7) | (Ebm7) (Ab7) | (Ebm7) (Ab7) | (Ebm7) Ebm7 Ab7 |
‖: Ebm7   Ab7 | Ebm7   Ab7 :‖

            Ebm7
Verse 1   Looking back on

Ab7   Ebm7   Ab7   Ebm7 Ab7 Ebm7 Ab7
When I was a little nap - py headed boy.

Ebm7   Ab7
Then my only worry

Ebm7   Ab7   Ebm7 Ab7 Eb7 Ab7
Was for Christmas what ___ would be my toy.

Bb7   C7   Fm7   Abm7
Even though we sometime would not get a thing,

Bb7   C7   Fm7   Bb+7
We were happy with the joy that they would bring.

Ebm7   Ab7
Sneaking out the back door,

  Ebm7   Ab7   Ebm7 Ab7 Ebm7 Ab7
To hang out with those hoodlum friends of mine,   ooh.

Ebm7   Ab7
Greeted at the back ___ door with,

  Ebm7   Ab7   Ebm7 Ab7 Ebm7 Ab7
"Boy, I thought I told you not ___ to go outside."

Bb7   C7   Fm7   Abm7
Try'n' your best to bring the water to your eyes,

Bb7   C7   Fm7   Bb+7
Thinkin' it might stop her from whoppin' your behind.

Chorus 1

Ebm7 Ab7 Ebm7   Ab7
I wish those days   could come back once more.

        Ebm7 Ab7 Ebm7   Ab7
Why did those days   ev - er have to go?

        Ebm7 Ab7 Ebm7   Ab7
I wish those days   could come back once more.

        Ebm7 Ab7 Ebm7   Ab7
Why did those days   ev - er have to go?

                Ebm7
'Cause I loved them so.

Verse 2

Ebm7   Ab7
Brother says he's tellin'

Ebm7   Ab7   Ebm7 Ab7 Ebm7 Ab7
'Bout you playin' doc - tor with that nurse.

Ebm7   Ab7
Just don't tell and I'll give you

Ebm7   Ab7   Ebm7   Ab7 Ebm7 Ab7
Anything you want ____ in this whole wide ___ world.

Bb7   C7   Fm7   Abm7
Mama gives you money for Sunday school,

Bb7   C7   Fm7   Bb+7
You trade just for candy after church is through.

Ebm7   Ab7
Smokin' cigarettes

    Ebm7   Ab7   Ebm7 Ab7   Ebm7 Ab7
And writtin' something nasty on the wall.   (You nasty boy.)

Ebm7   Ab7
Teachers send you to

    Ebm7   Ab7   Ebm7 Ab7 Ebm7 Ab7
The principal's office ____ down the hall.

Bb7   C7   Fm7   Abm7
You grow up and learn that kind of thing ain't right,

Bb7   C7   Fm7   Bb+7
But while you were doin' it, it sure felt outta sight.

Chorus 2

                Ebm7 Ab7 Ebm7   Ab7
I wish those days   could come back once more.

                Ebm7 Ab7 Ebm7   Ab7
Why did those days ev - er have to go?

                Ebm7 Ab7 Ebm7   Ab7
I wish those days   could come back once more.

                Ebm7 Ab7 Ebm7   Ab7
Why did those days ev - er have to go? Ooh, hoo.

Interlude | Ebm7 Ab7 | Ebm7 Ab7 | Ebm7 Ab7 | Ebm7 Ab7 |

Outro   ‖: Ebm7 Ab7 | Ebm7 Ab7 :‖ *Play 16 times and fade*

I'll Be There

Words and Music by Berry Gordy,
Hal Davis, Willie Hutch and Bob West

Melody:

You and I must make a pact.

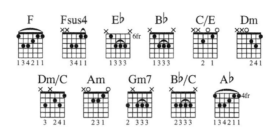

Intro

| F Fsus4 F | E♭ B♭ | F Fsus4 F | Fsus4 |

Verse 1

F   C/E
You and I must make a pact.

Dm   Dm/C   Am   B♭
We must bring sal - vation back.

Gm7   B♭/C   F
Where there is love, I'll ___ be there. (I'll be there.)

Verse 2

F   C/E
I'll reach out my hand to you,

Dm   Dm/C Am   B♭
I'll have faith in all you do.

Gm7   B♭/C   F
Just call my name and I'll ___ be there. (I'll be there.)

Bridge 1

       A♭   **E♭**
And oh,   I'll be there to comfort you,

       B♭
Build my world of dreams around you.

      F
I'm so glad that I found you.

A♭   **E♭**
  I'll be there with a love that's strong.

         B♭   **F**   **Fsus4**
I'll be your strength, I'll keep holdin' on.

                                             F
(Holdin' on, holdin' on, holdin' on.) Yes, I will. Yes, ____ I will.

Verse 3

     F   **C/E**
  Let me fill your heart ____ with joy and laughter.

Dm   **Dm/C** **Am**   **B♭**
  Together - ness,   well it's all I'm after.

       Gm7   **B♭/C**   **F**
When - ever you need me I'll ____ be there. (I'll be there.)

Verse 4

     F   **C/E**
  I'll be there to protect ____ you.

Dm   **Dm/C**   **Am**   **B♭**
  With an un - selfish love ____ that respects you.

Gm7   **B♭/C**   **F**
  Just call my name and I'll be there. (I'll be there.)

Bridge 2

       A♭   **E♭**
And oh,   I'll be there to comfort you,

       B♭
Build my world of dreams around you.

      F
I'm so glad that I found you.

A♭   **E♭**
  I'll be there with a love that's strong.

         B♭   **F**   **Fsus4**
I'll be your strength, I'll keep holdin' on. Ooh.

                                  F
(Holdin' on, holdin' on,) Yes, I will.

Verse 5

      F   C/E
If you should ever find someone new,

Dm   Dm/C Am   B♭
I know he better be good to you,

Gm7   B♭/C   F
'Cause if he ___ doesn't, I'll ___ be there. (I'll be there.)

Don't you know baby, yeah, yeah.

Outro

F   C/E Dm Dm/C   Am B♭
I'll be there, _____ I'll be there.

Gm7   B♭/C   F
Just call my name, I'll be there.

Just look over your shoulders, honey.

                 C/E Dm Dm/C   Am B♭
Ooh, I'll be there, _____ I'll be there.

           Gm7   B♭/C   F
When - ever you need me I'll ___ be there.

Don't you know baby, yeah, yeah.

F   C/E Dm Dm/C   Am B♭
I'll be there, _____ I'll be there.

Gm7   B♭/C   F
Just call my name, I'll ___ be there.

             C/E Dm Dm/C   Am B♭
I'll be there, _____ I'll be there.   ***Fade out***

If I Were Your Woman

Words and Music by
Clay McMurray, Pamela Sawyer
and Gloria Jones

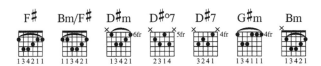

F#   Bm/F#   D#m   D#°7   D#7   G#m   Bm

Intro |F# |Bm/F# |F# |Bm/F# |

Verse 1

    D#m   D#°7
If I were your woman   and you were my man,

    F#   D#7
You'd have no other woman,   you'd be weak as a lamb.

    G#m   D#m
If you had the strength   to walk out that door,

    G#m   D#m
My love would overrule my sense,   and I'd call you back for more.

Chorus 1

              Bm
If I were your woman (If you were my woman.)

         D#m
If I were your woman (If you were my woman.)

             F#   Bm/F#
And you were my man. Mmm, ___ yeah.

Verse 2

D#m   D#°7
(Yeah!) She tears you down, darlin',   says you're nothing at all.

F#   D#7
But I'll pick you up, darlin',   when she lets you fall.

G#m   D#m
You're like a diamond,   but she treats you like glass.

G#m   Bm
Yet you beg her to love you,   but me you don't ask.

Chorus 2

           F#
If I were your woman (If you were my woman.)

         Bm/F#
If I were your woman (If you were my woman.)

         F#
If I were your woman (If you were my woman.)

       D#7
Here's what I do.

   Bm   F#   Bm/F#   F#   Bm/F#
I'd never no, no, stop loving you. Yeah,   yeah. Mmm.

Verse 3

D#m   D#°7
Life is so crazy   and love is unkind.

F#   D#7
Because she came first darlin',   will she hang on your mind?

G#m   D#m
You're a part of me   and you don't even know it.

G#m   D#m
I'm what you need, but I'm too afraid to show it.

Chorus 3

        F♯
If I were your woman (If you were my woman.)

        Bm/F♯
If I were your woman (If you were my woman.)

        F♯
If I were your woman (If you were my woman.)

        D♯7
Here's what I do.

Bm   **F♯**   **Bm/F♯**
Never no, no, no stop loving you. Oh, yeah.

        F♯   **D♯7**
If I were your woman, here's what I'd do.

   Bm   **F♯**
I'd never, never, never stop lovin' you.

Outro

        Bm/F♯   **F♯**
If I were your woman, your sweet lovin' woman.

                    Bm/F♯
(If you were my woman.) If I were your woman.

                    F♯
(If you were my woman.) I'll be your only woman.

                    Bm/F♯
(If you were my woman.) If I were your woman.

                       F♯
(If you were my woman.) There'd be no other woman.

                    Bm/F♯
(If you were my woman.) If I were your woman.   ***Fade out***

Lady Marmalade

Words and Music by
Bob Crewe and Kenny Nolan

(Hey, sis-ter, go sis-ter, soul sis-ter, go sis-ter.

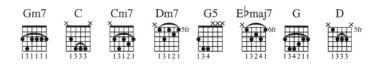

Gm7 C Cm7 Dm7 G5 E♭maj7 G D

Intro

| Gm7 C | | Gm7 C | |

Gm7   C
(Hey, sister, go sis - ter, soul sister, go sister.

Gm7   C
Hey, sister, go sis - ter, soul sister, go sister.)

Verse 1

           Gm7   C
He met Marmalade down in old ___ New Orleans,

Gm7   C
Struttin' her stuff on the street.

           Cm7   Dm7
She said, *"Hello, hey Joe, you wanna give it a go?"* Mm hmm.

Chorus 1

Gm7   C
Getcha, getcha, ya, ya, da, da.

Gm7   C
Getcha, getcha, ya, ya, here.

Gm7   C
Mocha chocolata, ya, ya.

Cm7 N.C.   G5
Creole Lady Marma - lade.

Gm7   C
Voulez vous coucher avec moi ce soir?

Gm7   C
Voulez vous coucher avec moi?

Verse 2

Gm7   C
Stayed in her boudoir while she ___ freshened up,

Gm7   C
   That boy drank all that magno - lia wine.

        Cm7   Dm7
On her black satin sheets, I swear ___ he started to freak.

Chorus 2   *Repeat Chorus 1*

Interlude

G5			Ebmaj7		
G			Ebmaj7		
D			

Verse 3

Gm7   C
   Seein' her skin, feeling silk - y smooth,

Gm7   C
Color of café au lait,

        Cm7   Dm7
Made the ___ savage beast inside roar until it cried,

  D
"More, more, more!"

Verse 4

Gm7   C
Now he's at home, doin' nine to five,

Gm7   C
Livin' his gray flannel life.

        Cm7   Dm7
But when he turns off the street, old ___ mem'ries scream,

D
More, more, more!

Chorus 3

```
Gm7                    C
Getcha, getcha, ya, ya, da, da.

Gm7                    C
Getcha, getcha, ya, ya, here.

Gm7              C
Mocha chocolata, ya, ya.

Cm7 N.C.              G5
Creole Lady Marma - lade.

Gm7                        C
Voulez vous coucher avec moi ce soir?

Gm7                      C
Voulez vous coucher avec moi?

Gm7                        C
Voulez vous coucher avec moi ce soir?

Cm7 N.C.              N.C.  Gm7
Creole Lady Marma - lade.

  Gm7 N.C.                  C N.C.
‖: Voulez vous coucher avec moi ce soir?

Gm7 N.C.               C N.C.
Voulez vous coucher avec moi?      :‖   *Play 4 times*
```

Outro

```
  Gm7                  C
‖: Getcha, getcha, ya, ya, da, da.

Gm7                  C
Getcha, getcha, ya, ya, here.

Gm7          C
Mocha chocolata, ya, ya.

Gm7                  C
Getcha, getcha, ya, ya, here.   :‖   *Repeat and fade*
```

Isn't She Lovely

Words and Music by
Stevie Wonder

Melody:

Is-n't she love - ly,

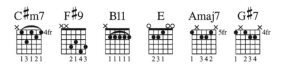

C#m7   F#9   B11   E   Amaj7   G#7

Intro

| N.C.(C#m7) | (F#9) | (B11) | (E) | |
‖: C#m7 | F#9 | B11 | E :‖ *Play 3 times*

Verse 1

     C#m7 F#9   B11   E
Isn't she lovely,   isn't she wonderful?

     C#m7 F#9   B11   E
Isn't she precious,   less than one minute old?

       Amaj7   G#7#5
I never thought ____ through love we'd be

     C#m7   F#9
Making one as lovely as she.

       B11   E N.C.
But isn't she lovely, made from love?

<table>
<tr><td>Verse 2</td><td>

C#m7 F#9   B11   E
Isn't she pretty,   truly the angels' best?

</td></tr>
</table>

C#m7 F#9   B11   E
Isn't she pretty,   truly the angels' best?

C#m7 F#9   B11   E
Boy, I'm so happy   we have been heaven blessed.

Amaj7   G#7#5
I can't believe ____ what God has done;

C#m7   F#9
Through us He's given life to one.

B11   E N.C.
But isn't she lovely, made from love?

Harmonica Solo 1   *Repeat Verse 1 (Instrumental)*

Verse 3

C#m7 F#9   B11   E
Isn't she lovely,   life and love are the same.

C#m7 F#9   B11   E
Life is A - isha,   the meaning of her name.

Amaj7   G#7#5
Londie, it could ____ not have been done

C#m7   F#9
Without you who conceived the one.

B11   E N.C.
That's so very lovely, made from love.

Harmonica Solo 2   *Repeat Verses till fade*

Just My Imagination
(Running Away with Me)

Words and Music by
Norman J. Whitfield
and Barrett Strong

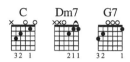

Intro

|N.C.　|C　|　|　|　|
|C Dm7 |　|C　Dm7 |　|

Verse 1

     C   Dm7   C Dm7
Each day through my window I ___ watch her as she passes by.

   C   Dm7   C Dm7
I say to myself, "You're such a lucky guy.

C   Dm7   C   Dm7
  To have a girl like her is truly a dream come true.

     C   Dm7   C   Dm7
Out of all the fellows in the world, she belongs ___ to you."

Chorus 1

     C   Dm7 C   Dm7
But it was just my imagination   runnin' away with me.

     C   Dm7   C   Dm7
It was just my imagina - tion runnin' a - way with me. ___ Ooh.

                    C   Dm7   C   Dm7
Verse 2   (Soon) Soon we'll be ____ married and raise a family. (Oh, yeah.)

              C   Dm7   C   Dm7
            A cozy little home out in the country with two child - ren, maybe three.

                      C Dm7   C   Dm7
            I tell you, I ____ can visual - ize it all.

                      C   Dm7   C   Dm7
            This couldn't be a dream, far too real it all ____ seems.

                              C   Dm7   C   Dm7
Chorus 2   But it was just my imagination once again, runnin' away with me.

                                    C   Dm7   C
            Tellin' you, it was just my imagina - tion runnin' a - way with me.

            C
Bridge   Ev'ry night on my knees I pray, ("Dear Lord,) hear my plea.

                                                            G7
            Don't ever let another take her love from me, or I would surely die."

                          C
            Mmm, (Her love is)   heavenly.

            When her arms enfold me, I hear a tender rhapsody.

            But in reality, she doesn't even know me.

              C   Dm7   C
Chorus 3   (Just my imagination) Once again, runnin' away with me.

            Dm7   C   Dm7   C
            Oh, tell you it was just my imagina - tion runnin' a - way with me.

            Dm7
            I'll never, never, no, no can't forget her.

            C   Dm7   C
            (Just my imagination) Yeah, yeah, yeah, yeah. (Runnin' away with me.)

            Dm7 C   Dm7   C
            Ooh, just my imagina - tion runnin' a -way with me.   *Fade out*

Living for the City

Words and Music by
Stevie Wonder

Melody:

A boy is born _ in hard time Mis - sis - sip - pi,

Tune down 1/2 step:
(low to high) Eb - Ab - Db - Gb - Bb - Eb

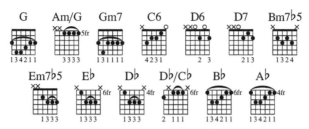

Intro	‖: G Am/G Gm7 | Am/G :‖	

Verse 1

G   Am/G Gm7   Am/G
A boy is born   in hard time Missis - sippi,

G   Am/G Gm7   Am/G
Surrounded by   four walls that ain't so pret - ty.

G   Am/G Gm7   Am/G
His parents give   him love and affect - tion

G   Am/G Gm7
To keep him strong,   movin' in the right direction.

Chorus 1

C6   D6   D7   G Am/G Gm7 Am/G
Livin' just enough, just e - nough for the cit - y.

Verse 2

G   Am/G   Gm7   Am/G
His father works,   some days for fourteen hours,

G   Am/G   Gm7   Am/G
And you can bet   he barely makes a dol - lar.

G   Am/G   Gm7   Am/G
His mother goes,   scrub the floors for man - y,

G   Am/G   Gm7   Am/G
And you best believe   she hardly gets a penny.

Chorus 2   *Repeat Chorus 1*

Interlude 1 |¾ Bm7♭5 | Em7♭5 | E♭ | D♭ | D♭/C♭ |
                | B♭ |²₄ A♭ |⁴₄ G | |

Verse 3

G   Am/G   Gm7   Am/G
His sister's black,   but she is sho 'nuff pretty.

G   Am/G   Gm7   Am/G
Her skirt is short,   but Lord, her legs are stur - dy.

G   Am/G   Gm7   Am/G
To walk to school,   she's got to get up ear - ly.

G   Am/G   Gm7
Her clothes are old,   but never are they dirty.

Chorus 3   *Repeat Chorus 1*

Verse 4

G   Am/G Gm7   Am/G
Her brother's smart,   he's got more sense than many.

G   Am/G Gm7   Am/G
His patience long,   but soon he won't have an - y.

G   Am/G Gm7   Am/G
To find a job   is like a haystack nee - dle,

G   Am/G Gm7   Am/G
'Cause where he lives,   they don't use colored people.

Chorus 4

          C6
Livin' just enough,

D6   D7   G Am/G Gm7 Am/G G Am/G Gm7
Just e - nough for the cit - y.

Interlude 2 |¾ Bm7b5 |Em7b5 |Eb |Db |Db/Cb |

                 |Bb |²⁄₄Ab |⁴⁄₄G | |

                 | G   Am/G Gm7 | Am/G |

Outro

          G   Am/G Gm7   Am/G
||: Livin' just e - nough for the city. Oh.   :|| *Repeat and fade*
                                                  w/ lead vocal ad lib.

Money
(That's What I Want)

Words and Music by
Berry Gordy and Janie Bradford

Melody:

The best _ things in   life are   free. _

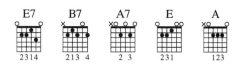

E7   B7   A7   E   A
2314   213 4   2 3   231   123

Intro

| E7 | | | | |
| B7 | A7 | E7 | B7 | |

Verse 1

   E   A   E
The best things in life are free.

But you can keep them for the birds and bees.

            A7
Now give me mon   -   ey.
           (That's   what I want.)

           E7
That's what I want. (That's what I want.)

           B7   A7
That's what I want,   yeah.
           (That's what I   want.)

E7   B7
That's what I want.

Verse 2

```
            E                        A    E
            Your lovin' give me a thrill.

        But your lovin' don't pay my bills.
                A7
        Now give me mon    -    ey.
                        (That's      what I want.)

                    E7
        That's what I want. (That's what I want.)
                    B7           A7
        That's what I want,           yeah.
                        (That's what I    want.)

        E7                B7
            That's what I want.
```

Verse 3

```
            E                           A    E
            Money don't get ev'rything it's true.

        What it don't get I can't use.
                A7
        Now give me mon    -    ey.
                        (That's      what I want.)

                    E7
        That's what I want. (That's what I want.)
                    B7           A7
        That's what I want,           yeah.
                        (That's what I    want.)

        E7                B7
            That's what I want.
```

Solo   *Repeat Intro*

Verse 4   *Repeat Verse 3*

                                        E7
Verse 5   Well, now give me money. (That's what I want.)

                                                              A7
                       A lotta money.   Wow, yeah. I wanna be free.
                                 (That's   what I want.)

                       (That's what I want.)

                            E7
                       Whole lot - ta money.
                                 (That's what I want.)

                            B7   **A7**
                       That's what I want,   yeah.
                                        (That's what I   want.)
                       E7   **B7**
                            That's what I want.

                                        E7
Verse 6   Well, now give me money. (That's what I want.)

                                                              A7
                       A lotta money.   Wow, yeah. You know I need mon - ey.
                                 (That's   what I want.)

                                            E7
                            Oh,   now give me money.
                       (That's what I want.)   (That's what I want.)

                            B7   **A7**
                       That's what I want,   yeah.
                                        (That's what I   want.)

                       E7
                            That's what I want.

Mercy, Mercy Me
(The Ecology)

Words and Music by
Marvin Gaye

Melody:

Whoa, __ ah, __ mer - cy, mer - cy me. __

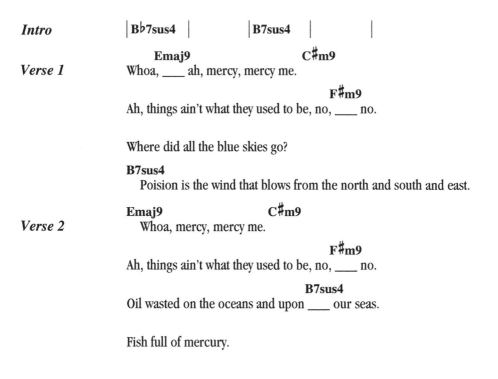

Bb7sus4	B7sus4	Emaj9	C#m9	F#m9	Fmaj9	Dm9	Gm9	C7sus4	Bbm9

Intro | Bb7sus4 | | B7sus4 | | |

Verse 1
       Emaj9   **C#m9**
Whoa, ____ ah, mercy, mercy me.

                                        F#m9
Ah, things ain't what they used to be, no, ____ no.

Where did all the blue skies go?

B7sus4
  Poision is the wind that blows from the north and south and east.

Verse 2
  Emaj9   **C#m9**
  Whoa, mercy, mercy me.

                                        F#m9
Ah, things ain't what they used to be, no, ____ no.

                                B7sus4
Oil wasted on the oceans and upon ____ our seas.

Fish full of mercury.

Verse 3	**Emaj9** **C#m9** Ah, ___ oh, mercy, mercy me.

Verse 3

           Emaj9   **C#m9**

Ah, ___ oh, mercy, mercy me.

                                     F#m9

Ah, things ain't what they used to be, no, ___ no.

                         B7sus4

Radiation underground and in the ___ sky.

                                Emaj9

Animals and birds who live nearby are dying.

Verse 4

                      C#m9

Oh, mercy, mercy me.

                          F#m9

Ah, things ain't what they used ___ to be.

                         B7sus4

What about this overcrowded land?

How much more abuse from man can she stand?

Interlude   *Repeat Verse 1 w/ vocal ad lib.*

Sax Solo | **Fmaj9** | | **Dm9** | |

                     | **Gm9** | | **C7sus4** | |

Outro ||: **B♭m9** | :|| *Repeat and fade*

My Cherie Amour

Words and Music by Stevie Wonder,
Sylvia Moy and Henry Cosby

La, la, la, la, __ la, la.

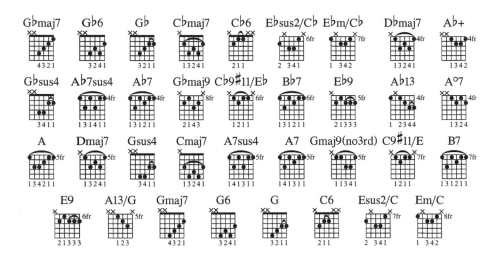

Intro

N.C. | Gbmaj7 Gb6 Gb | Cbmaj7 Cb6 Cbmaj7 | Ebsus2/Cb Ebm/Cb |

| Dbmaj7 N.C. Gbmaj7 Gb6 Gb Cbmaj7

La, la, la,   la, la, la.

Cb6 Cbmaj7 Ebsus2/Cb Ebm/Cb Dbma7

La,   la,   la,   la, la,   la.

Chorus 1

Ab+   Dbmaj7 Gbsus4   Cbmaj7 Ab7sus4 Ab7

My Che - rie Amour, lovely as a summer day.

Dbmaj7 Gbsus4   Cbmaj7 Ab7sus4 Ab7

My Che - rie Amour, distant as the Milky Way.

Gbmaj9 Ab7sus4 Ab7   Cb9#11/Eb

My Che - rie Amour, pretty little one that I ____ adore,

Bb7   Eb9

You're the only girl my heart ____ beats for.

Ab13   Ab7   Dbmaj7

How I wish that you ____ were mine.

Verse 1

A°7   Dbmaj7 Gbsus4   Cbmaj7 Ab7sus4
In a café or   sometimes on a crowded street,

Ab7   Dbmaj7   Gbsus4   Cbmaj7 Ab7sus4 Ab7
I've been near you but you never noticed me.

          Gbmaj9 Ab7sus4   Ab7   Cb9#11/Eb
My Che - rie Amour, won't you tell me how could you ___ ignore,

Bb7   Eb9
That behind that little smile ___ I wore,

Ab13   Ab7   Dbmaj7
How I wish that you were ___ mine.

Interlude

   N.C. Gbmaj7 Gb6 Gb Cbmaj7
‖: La, la, la,   la,   la,   la.

Cb6 Cbmaj7 Ebsus2/Cb Ebm/Cb Dbma7
La,   la,   la,   la, la,   la.   :‖

Verse 2

A   Dmaj7   Gsus4   Cmaj7
Maybe someday, you'll see my face among the crowd.

A7sus4 A7   Dmaj7   Gsus4   Cmaj7 A7sus4
May -   be someday, I'll share your little distant cloud.

    A7   Gmaj9(no3rd) A7sus4   A7   C9#11/E
Oh, ___ Che - rie Amour,   pretty little one that I ___ adore

      B7   E9
You're ___ the only girl my heart ___ beats for.

A13/G   A7   Dmaj7
How I wish that you were mine.

Outro

   N.C. Gmaj7 G6 G Cmaj7
‖: La, la, la,   la,   la, la.

C6 Cmaj7 Esus2/C Em/C Dmaj7
La,   la,   la,   la, la,   la. :‖ *Repeat and fade*

My Girl

Words and Music by
William "Smokey" Robinson and Ronald White

Melody:

I've _ got sun - shine _____

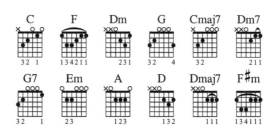

Intro

| N.C.(C) | | | | |

Verse 1

N.C. (C) C   F   C   F
I've got   sunshine ___ on a cloud - y day.

    C   F   C   F
When it's cold outside, ___ I've got the month of May.

Chorus 1

C Dm   F   G
I guess you'd say,

C   Dm   F   G
What can make me feel this way?

Cmaj7   Dm7   G7   Dm7
My girl, (My girl, my girl.) Talkin' 'bout___ my girl, (My girl.)

Verse 2

  G7   C   F   C   F
I've ___ got so much honey, the bees envy me.

    C   F   C   F
I've got a sweeter song ___ than the birds in the trees.

Chorus 2

         C Dm F   G
Well, I guess you'd say,

C   Dm   F   G
What can make me feel this way?

Cmaj7   Dm7   G7
My girl, (My girl, my girl.) Talkin' 'bout   my girl, (My girl.)

Dm7 G7 N.C.(C)
Oo.

Interlude

| C | F | C | F | |
| Dm | G | Em | A N.C. | |

Verse 3

         D   **G**   **D G**
I don't need no money, ___ fortune, or fame.

        D   **G**   **D**   **G**
I got all the riches, baby, ___ one man ___ can claim.

Chorus 3

        D Em G   A
Well, I guess you'd say,

D   Em   G   A
What can make me feel this way?

Dmaj7   Em
My girl, (My girl, my girl.) talkin' 'bout ___ my girl.

A   G F♯m Em Dmaj7
(My girl,   talkin' 'bout my girl.)

                                       Em
I got sunshine on a cloudy day with my ___ girl.

     A   G   **F♯m Em   Dmaj7**
I've even got the month ___ of May with ___ my girl.

Talkin' 'bout.   ***Fade out***

My Guy

Words and Music by
William "Smokey" Robinson

Melody:

Noth-ing you could say could tear ___ me a - way

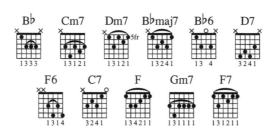

Bb   Cm7   Dm7   Bbmaj7   Bb6   D7
1333   13121   13121   13241   13 4   3241

F6   C7   F   Gm7   F7
1314   3241   134211   131111   131211

Intro | Bb | | | Cm7 Dm7 |

Verse 1
    Bbmaj7   **Bb6**   **Bbmaj7**   **Bb6**
Nothing you could say could tear ___ me a - way

       Bbmaj7 **Bb6** **Bbmaj7** **Bb6**
From my ___ guy.

    Bbmaj7   **Bb6**   **Bbmaj7**   **Bb6**
Nothing you could do 'cause I'm ___ stuck like glue

      D7
To my ___ guy.

     Cm7   **F6**   **Cm7**   **F6**
I'm sticking to my guy like a stamp to a letter,

      Cm7   **F6**   **Cm7 N.C.**
Like birds of a feather we   stick together.

    Bb   **Bbmaj7**   **C7**   **F**
I'm tellin' you from the start I can't ___ be torn a - part

           Bb   **Cm7 Dm7**
From my ___ guy.

Verse 2

Bbmaj7   Bb6   Bbmaj7 Bb6
Nothing you could do could make ___ me un - true

  Bbmaj7 Bb6 Bbmaj7 Bb6
To my ___ guy. (My ___ guy.)

Bbmaj7   Bb6   Bbmaj7 Bb6
Nothing you could buy could make ___ me tell a lie

   D7
To my ___ guy. (My guy, my guy, my guy.)

 Cm7 F6 Cm7   F6
I gave my guy my word of honor

Cm7 F6 Cm7 N.C.
To be faithful, and I'm gonna.

  Bb   Bbmaj7   C7   F
You best be be - lieving I won't ___ be de - ceiving

   Bb   Cm7 Dm7
My ___ guy.

Bridge

   Cm7   F   Cm7   F
As a matter of o - pinion I think he's tops.

Cm7   F   Bb
My opinion is he's the cream of the crop,

   Gm7   Dm7 Gm7 Dm7
As a matter of taste, ___ to be exact,

C7   F
He's my ideal, as a matter of fact.

Verse 3

   Bbmaj7 Bb6   Bbmaj7 Bb6
No musclebound man could take my hand

   Bbmaj7 Bb6 Bbmaj7 Bb6
From my ___ guy. (My ___ guy.)

   Bbmaj7 Bb6   Bbmaj7 Bb6
No handsome face ___ could ever take the place

   D7
Of my ___ guy. (My guy, my guy, my guy.)

  Cm7 F Cm7   F
He may not be a movie star,

     Cm7   F Cm7 N.C.
But when it comes to bein' happy, we are.

     Bb   Gm7   C7   F7
There's not a man today ___ who could take me a - way

    Bbmaj7 Bb6 Cm7 Dm7
From my ___ guy.

Interlude   *Repeat Intro*

             B♭maj7   **B♭6**   **B♭maj7**   **B♭6**

Verse 4   No musclebound man could take my hand

                B♭maj7 **B♭6** **B♭maj7** **B♭6**

From my ____ guy.   (My ____ guy.)

           B♭maj7   **B♭6**   **B♭maj7**   **B♭6**

No handsome face ____ that ever take the place

          D7

Of my ____ guy. (My guy, my guy, my guy.)

        Cm7   **F**   **Cm7**   **F**

He may not be a movie star,

              Cm7   **F**   **Cm7 N.C.**

But when it comes to bein' happy,   we are.

            N.C. **(B♭)**   **(Gm7)**   **(C7)**   **(F7)**

There's not a man today ____ who could take me a - way

               B♭maj7 **B♭6** **Cm7**   **Dm7**

From my ____ guy.   (What you say?)

               N.C. (B♭) (Gm7)   **(C7)**   **(F7)**

Outro   There's not a man today ____ who could take me a - way

               B♭maj7 **B♭6** **Cm7**   **Dm7**

From my ____ guy.   (Tell me more.)

               N.C. (B♭) (Gm7)   **(C7)**   **(F7)**

There's not a man today ____ who could take me a - way

               B♭maj7   **B♭6** **Cm7**   **Dm7**

From my ____ guy.   (What's that?)

There's not a man today…   ***Fade out***

Never Can Say Goodbye

Words and Music by
Clifton Davis

Melody:

Nev-er can __ say good-bye. __   No, no, no, no, I

D   Em7   Em7/A   Dmaj7   Am7/D   Gmaj7   E/D   Eb/D

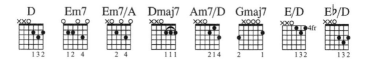

Intro

| D | Em7 | | |

Chorus 1

Em7   Em7/A
Never can say goodbye.

No, no, no, no, I

Em7   Em7/A
Never can say goodbye.

Verse 1

Dmaj7
Even though the pain and heartache

Am7/D
Seem to follow me wherever I go.

Dmaj7
Though I try and try to hide my feelings,

Am7/D
They always seem to show.

Dmaj7
Then you try to say you're leaving me,

Am7/D
And I always have to say no

Gmaj7   Em7
Tell me why, is it so?

Chorus 2

      Em7   **Em7/A**
That I   never can say goodbye.

No, no, no, no, I

Em7   **Em7/A**
  Never can say goodbye.

Verse 2

    Dmaj7
Every time I think I've had enough

    Am7/D
I start heading for the door.

    Dmaj7
There's a very strange vibration

    Am7/D
That pierces me right to the core.

    Dmaj7
It says turnaround you fool,

    Am7/D
You know you love her more and more.

    Gmaj7 **Em7**
Tell me why, is it so?

Don't want to let you go.

Bridge

Dmaj7   **Am7/D**
  I never can say goodbye, ___ girl.

    E/D **E♭/D**   **D**
Ooh, ooh, ba - by, I never can say good - bye.

No, no, no, no, no, no, no, no, no, no, no.

Dmaj7   **Am7/D**
  Oh, I never can say goodbye, ___ girl.

    E/D   **E♭/D**   **D**
Ooh, ooh,   ooh, never can say good - bye.

No, no, no, no, no, no, no, no, no.

Chorus 3   Repeat Chorus 1

                     Dmaj7

Verse 2   I keep thinking that our problems

                     Am7/D

           Soon are all gonna work out.

                     Dmaj7

           But there's that same unhappy feeling,

                     Am7

           And there's that anguish, there's that doubt.

                     Dmaj7

           It's the same old dizzy hangup

                     Am7/D

           Can't do with you or without.

                     Gmaj7   Em7

           Tell me why, is it so?

           Don't want to let you go.

           Dmaj7   **Am7/D**

Outro   I never can say goodbye, ___ girl.

                   E/D   E♭/D   **D**

           Ooh, ooh, ba - by, I never can say good - bye.

           No, no, no, no, no, no, no, no, no.

           Dmaj7   **Am7/D**

           Oh, I never, never say goodbye, ___ girl.

           E/D   **E♭/D**   **D**

           Ooh,   hey, I never, never say good - bye.

           No, no, no, no, no, no, no, no, no.

           Dmaj7   **Am7/D**

           I never, never say goodbye, ___ girl.

                   E/D   E♭/D   **D**

           Ooh, ooh, ba - by, I never, never say good - bye.

           No, no, no, no, no, no, no, no, no.   *Fade out*

Nowhere to Run

Words and Music by Lamont Dozier,
Brian Holland and Edward Holland

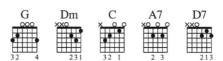

Intro

| N.C.(G) | | |

Chorus 1

    G   Dm   C
Nowhere to run ___ to, baby,

    G   Dm C
Nowhere to hide.

    G   Dm   C
Got nowhere to run ___ to, baby,

    G   Dm C
Nowhere to hide.

Verse 1

    G   Dm   C
It's not love I'm running from,

    G   Dm   C
It's the heartbreak I know will come.

    G   Dm   C
'Cause I know you're no good for me,

    G   Dm   C
But you've become a part of me.

        G N.C. (G)
Ev'ry - where I go, your face I see.

Ev'ry step I take, you take with me.

GUITAR CHORD SONGBOOK

Chorus 2

           G   Dm   C
Yeah, ___ nowhere to run ___ to, baby,

G   Dm   C
Nowhere to hide.

G   Dm   C
Got nowhere to run ___ to, baby,

G   Dm C
Nowhere to hide.

Bridge 1

A7
I know you're no good for me,

D7
But free of you I'll never be, no.

Verse 2

G   Dm   C
Each night as I sleep,

G   Dm   C
Into my heart you creep.

G   Dm   C
I wake up feelin' sorry I met ___ you.

G   Dm   C
Hoping soon that I'll forget you.

          G N.C. (G)
When I look in the mirror to comb my hair,

I see your face just a smilin' there.

Chorus 3

G   Dm C
Nowhere to run, ___ nowhere to

      G   Dm C
Hide ___ from you, ba - by.

G   Dm   C
Got nowhere to run ___ to baby,

G   Dm C
Nowhere to hide.

Bridge 2

A7
I know you're no good for me,

D7
But you've become a part of me.

Verse 3

G   Dm C
How can I fight ____ a lov - er

G   Dm C
 That shouldn't be

     G Dm C
When it's so deep, so deep,

G   Dm C
 Deep inside of me?

    G N.C. (G)
My love reaches so high I can't get over it.

It's so wide I can't get around it, no.

Chorus 4

G   Dm C
 Nowhere to run, ____ nowhere to

   G   Dm C
Hide ____ from you, ba - by.

G   Dm   C
 Just can't get a - way from you, baby,

G   Dm C
 No matter how I try.

Bridge 3

A7
I know you're no good for me,

D7
But free of you I'll never be.

Outro

G   Dm C
 Nowhere to run ____ to, baby,

G   Dm C
 Nowhere to hide.

  G   Dm C
‖: Got nowhere to run ____ to, baby

G   Dm C
 Nowhere to hide. :‖ *Repeat and fade*

Reach Out, I'll Be There

Words and Music by Brian Holland,
Lamont Dozier and Edward Holland

Melody:

Now, if you feel that you can't go on ___

(Capo 1st fret)

Dsus4 Dm Dsus2 A Gm7 F C A7 E°7 D

Intro

Dsus4 Dm	Dsus4 Dm Dsus2 Dm
A	
Dsus4 Dm	Dsus4 Dm Dsus2 Dm
A	

Verse 1

     A   Gm7   F   C
Now, if you feel that you can't ___ go on

          Gm7   F C
Because all your hope is gone.

          Gm7   F   C
And your life is filled with much ___ con - fusion,

          Gm7   F   C
Until happiness is just an il - lusion.

             Gm7   F   C
And your world ___ around is crum - bling down. Darling.

     F
(Reach out.) *Hello girl, reach on out for me.*

     A7   E°7 N.C.
(Reach out.) *Reach out for me.*   *Ha!*

Chorus 1

```
       A     D         Dsus4 Dm          Dsus2 Dm   A
       I'll be there with a love _____ that will shel - ter you.

             D         Dsus4 Dm          Dsus2 Dm       A
       I'll be there with a love _____ that will see     you through.
```

Verse 2

```
                 Gm7         F     C
       When you feel lost and about to give up,

                 Gm7         F     C
       'Cause your best just ain't good e - nough.

             Gm7             F     C
       And you feel the world has grown cold,

             Gm7       F     C
       And you're drifting all on your own.

             Gm7       F C
       And you need a hand to hold. Darling.

       F
       (Reach out.) *Hello girl, reach out for me.*

       A7                          E°7 N.C.
       (Reach out.) *Reach out for me.      Ha!*
```

Chorus 2

```
       A     D     Dsus4 Dm   Dsus2 Dm A
       I'll be there to love _____ and com - fort you.

                 D     Dsus4 Dm   Dsus2 Dm       A
       And I'll be there to cher - ish and care _____ for you.

                 D     Dsus4 Dm Dsus2 Dm A
       (I'll be there to al - ways see   you through.)

                 D     Dsus4 Dm Dsus2 Dm B♭
       (I'll be there to love    and com - fort you.
```

                    Gm7   **F   C**
Verse 3   I can tell the way you hang your head,

                            Gm7   **F**   **C**
                Your without love _____ now, now you're a - fraid.

                            Gm7   **F   C**
                And through your tears you'll look a - round,

                        Gm7   **F   C**
                But there's no _____ peace of mind to be found.

                I know what you're thinkin',

                Gm7   **F   C**
                   You're a loner,   no love of your own. But darlin'.

                F
                (Reach out.) *Come on girl, reach out for me.*

                A7   **E°7 N.C.**
                (Reach out.)   *Just look over your shoulder.*

                A   D   Dsus4 Dm   Dsus Dm   A
Chorus 3   I'll be there to give   you all the love _____ you need.

                            D
                And I'll be there,

                        Dsus4 Dm   Dsus2 Dm   A
                You can al - ways de - pend on me.   *Fade out*

Ooo Baby Baby

Words and Music by
William "Smokey" Robinson and Warren Moore

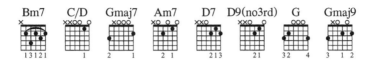

Intro |Bm7 |C/D |Bm7 |C/D |

Ooo, la, la, la, la,

Verse 1

       Gmaj7   **Am7**
I did you wrong; my heart went out to play,

          Bm7
And in the game, I lost you.

         Am7   **D7**
What a price to pay. I'm cryin'

Chorus 1

       Gmaj7 **Am7**
Ooo, ____ baby, baby.

       Gmaj7 **Am7**
Ooo, ____ baby, baby.

Verse 2

       Gmaj7   **Am7**
Mis-takes, I know I've made a few,

         Bm7
But I'm only human;

              Am7   **D7**
You've made mistakes too. I'm cryin'.

	Gmaj7 Am7
Chorus 2	Ooo, ___ baby, baby.

Gmaj7   Am7
Ooo, ___ baby, baby.

Gmaj7   Am7
Ooo, ___ baby, baby.

Gmaj7
Ooo, ___ ooh, baby, baby.

Bridge

Bm7   **D9(no 3rd)**
I'm just a-bout at the end of my rope.

        Bm7   **D9(no 3rd)**
But I can't stop tryin', I can't give up hope

       G   **Am7**
'Cause I feel ___ someday I'll hold you near.

   Bm7   **Am7**
Whisper I still love you until that day is here.

  D7
Ooo, I'm cryin'.

Chorus 3

Gmaj7   Am7
Ooo, ___ baby, baby.

Gmaj7   Am7
Ooo, ___ baby, baby.

Gmaj7   Am7
Ooo, ___ baby, baby.

Gmaj7   Am7   Gmaj9
Ooo, ___ ooo, baby, baby. Ooo.

Please Mr. Postman

Words and Music by Robert Bateman, Georgia Dobbins,
William Garrett, Freddie Gorman and Brian Holland

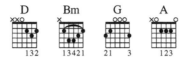

Intro

    D
(Wait.) Oh yes, wait a minute, Mister Postman.

Bm
(Wait.) Wait, Mister Postman.

Chorus 1

    D
    Mister Postman look and see,

Bm
    Is there a letter in your bag for me?

G
    'Cause it's been a mighty long time,

A
    Since I heard from this boyfriend of mine.

Verse 1

D
There must be some word today,

Bm
From my boyfriend so far away.

G
Please, Mister Postman, look and see;

A
Is there a letter, a letter for me?

D
I've been standing here waiting, Mister Postman,

Bm
So, so patiently,

G
For just a card or just a letter,

A
Saying he's returning home to me.

Chorus 2   *Repeat Chorus 1*

Verse 2

D
So many days you've passed me by;

Bm
You saw the tears standing in my eyes.

G
You wouldn't stop to make me feel better

A
By leaving me a card or a letter.

D
Please, Mister Postman, look and see;

Bm
Is there a letter, oh yeah, in your bag for me?

G
You know it's been so long,

A
Yeah, since I heard from this boyfriend of mine.

Outro   *Repeat Chorus 1 till fade*

Reach Out and Touch
(Somebody's Hand)

Words and Music by
Nickolas Ashford and Valerie Simpson

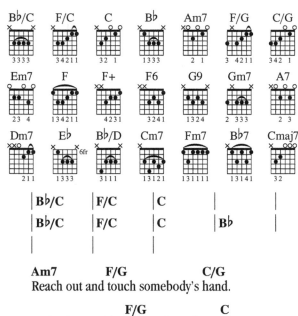

Intro

Bb/C	F/C	C		
Bb/C	F/C	C	Bb	

Chorus 1

Am7   F/G   C/G
Reach out and touch somebody's hand.

                F/G   C
Make this world a better place if you can.

Am7   F/G   C
Reach out and touch somebody's hand.

Am7   F/G
Make this world a better place.

Verse 1

       Em7   Am7   C   F
If you can, just try, take a little time out of your busy day

  F+   F6   G9   Em7
To give en - couragement to someone who's lost the way.

Am7   C   F
  Or, would I be talking to a stone

  F+   F6   G9   Gm7   A7
If I asked you to share a problem that's not your own?

C   F   Am7   Dm7
We can change things if we start giving.

Chorus 2

N.C.   F/G   C/G
Why don't you reach out and touch somebody's hand.

              F/G   C
Make this world a better place if you can.

Am7   F/G   C
Reach out and touch somebody's hand.

Am7   F/G
Make this world a better place.

Verse 2

     Em7   Am7   C   F
If you can, just try. If you see an old friend on the street,

       F+   F6   G9   Em7
And he's down, re - member his shoes could fit your feet.

Am7   C   F
   Try a little kindness and you will see

    F+   F6   G9   Gm7
It's something that comes   very nat'ral - ly.

A7   C   F   Am7   Dm7
  We ____ can change things if we start giving.

Chorus 3

N.C.   Am7
Why don't you, why don't you,

       F/G   C Bb
Reach out and touch somebody's hand?

Bridge

Eb	Bb/D	Cm7	Fm7	
	Bb7	Eb	Bb/D	
Cm7	Fm7	Cmaj7	C	

Outro

   Am7   F/G   C
‖: Reach out and touch somebody's hand.

Am7   F/G   C
Make this world a better place if you can. :‖ *Repeat and fade*
                                           w/ vocal ad lib.

Ribbon in the Sky

Words and Music by
Stevie Wonder

Melody:

Oh __ so long ____ for this night I prayed, _

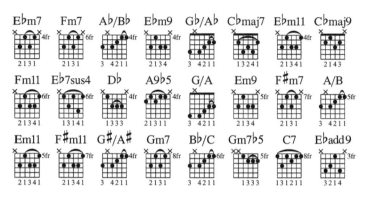

Intro

‖: Ebm7 |Fm7 Ab/Bb |Ebm7 |Fm7   Ab/Bb :‖
|Ebm7 |Fm7 Ab/Bb |Ebm9 Gb/Ab |Cbmaj7 Gb/Ab |

Verse 1

    Ebm7   Fm7   Ab/Bb
Oh, ___ so long for this night I prayed,

     Ebm7   Fm7   Ab/Bb
That a star would guide you my way.

    Ebm7   Fm7 Ab/Bb
To ___ share with me this special day,

      Ebm11   Gb/Ab   Cbmaj9 Gb/Ab
Where a ribbon's in the sky ___ for our love.

Verse 2

    Ebm7   Fm11   Ab/Bb
If ___ allowed, may I touch your hand?

     Ebm11   Fm11   Ab/Bb
And if pleased, may I once a - gain?

    Ebm11   Fm11 Ab/Bb
So ___ that you too will under - stand,

     Ebm11   Gb/Ab   Db
There's a ribbon in the sky ___ for our love.

Verse 3

Ebm7 Fm11 Ab/Bb
Do, _____ do.

Ebm11   Fm11
Mm, do, do, do, do, do, do, do, do, do, do, do, do, do, do, do,

Ab/Bb
Do, do, do, do.

Ebm11 Fm11 Ab/Bb
Mm, ___ do, ___ do, ___ dum.

Ebm11 Gb/Ab   A9b5 G/A
Do, _____ mm.

Verse 4

Em9   F#m7 A/B
This is not a coinci - dence,

Em11   F#m11 A/B
And far more than a lucky   chance.

Em11   F#m7   A/B
But what is that was always meant,

Em11   G/A   G#/A#
Is our ribbon in the sky ___ for our love, love.

Verse 5

Fm11   Gm7   Bb/C
We can't lose ___ with God ___ on our side.

Fm11   Gm7   Bb/C
We'll find strength in each tear we cry.

Fm11   Gm7   Bb/C
From now on it will be ___ you and I,

Fm11   Ab/Bb   Gm7b5   C7
And our ribbon in the sky, ___ ribbon ___ in the sky,

Fm7   Ab/Bb   Fm11
A rib - bon in the sky   for our love.

Verse 6

Gm7 Bb/C
Ah, ooh, ___ do.

Fm11
Mm, do, do, do, do, do, do, do, do, do, do, do, do, do, do,

Gm7   Bb/C
Do, do, do, do, ___ mm.

Fm11 Gm7
Mm, _____ mm.

Fm11   Ab/Bb   Ebadd9
There's a rib - bon in the sky   for our love.

Shop Around

Words and Music by Berry Gordy
and William "Smokey" Robinson

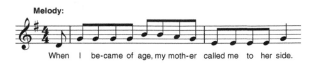

Melody:

When I be-came of age, my moth-er called me to her side.

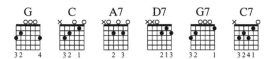

G   C   A7   D7   G7   C7

Intro

       G   C
When I became of age, my mother called me to her side.

          A7   D7
She said, "Son, you're growing up now, pretty soon you'll take a bride."

Verse 1

          G7   C7
And then she said, "Just because you've be - come a young man now,

G7   C7
There's still some things that you don't understand now.

G7   C7
Before you ask some girl for her hand now,

G7   C7
Keep your freedom for as long as you can now."

Chorus 1

A7   D7 N.C.   G7
My Mama told me you better shop a - round,

   C7   G7   D7
Oh yeah, you better shop a - round.   Ah.

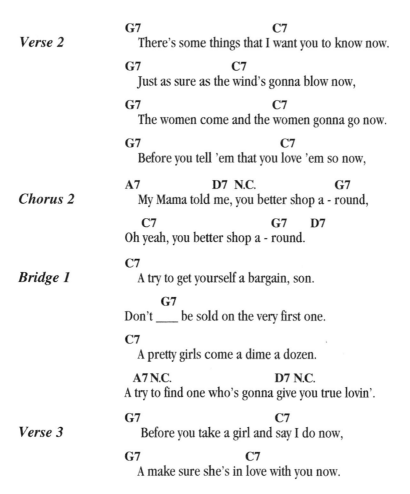

Verse 2

G7   C7
There's some things that I want you to know now.

G7   C7
Just as sure as the wind's gonna blow now,

G7   C7
The women come and the women gonna go now.

G7   C7
Before you tell 'em that you love 'em so now,

Chorus 2

A7   D7 N.C.   G7
My Mama told me, you better shop a - round,

      C7   G7   D7
Oh yeah, you better shop a - round.

Bridge 1

C7
A try to get yourself a bargain, son.

        G7
Don't ___ be sold on the very first one.

C7
A pretty girls come a dime a dozen.

A7 N.C.   D7 N.C.
A try to find one who's gonna give you true lovin'.

Verse 3

G7   C7
Before you take a girl and say I do now,

G7   C7
A make sure she's in love with you now.

| | A7   D7 N.C.   G7 N.C. G7 N.C. |
| **Chorus 3** | My Mama told me you better shop a - round. |

Sax Solo

	G7		C7		G7		C7		
	G7		C7		G7 N.C.		C7		

Oh, yeah.

Bridge 2   *Repeat Bridge 1*

                                   G7   C7
Verse 4   Before you take a girl and say I do now,

                    G7   C7
        Make sure she's in love with you now.

                    G7   C7
        Make sure that her love is true now,

                    G7   C7
        I hate to see you feelin' sad and blue now.

                    A7   D7 N.C.   G7
Chorus 4   My Mama told me you better shop a - round.

                    C7   G7
Outro   Ah, huh, don't let the first one get ya.

                           C7   G7
        ‖: Oh, no ___ 'cause I don't wanna see 'em with you

                    C7   G7
        Ah, huh, before you let 'em hold ___ you tight. :‖ *Repeat and fade*
                                                                  w/ vocal ad lib.

Signed, Sealed, Delivered I'm Yours

Words and Music by Stevie Wonder,
Syreeta Wright, Lee Garrett
and Lula Mae Hardaway

Melody:

Like a fool I went and stayed too long.

(Capo 1st fret)

E   E7   E6   E5   Esus4   E*   C#m7   A   A/B   E7*

Intro | E E7 E6 E5 | Esus4 E* | | E E7 E6 E5 | Esus4 E* |

Hey, hey.   Oh yeah, ba - by.

Verse 1
E*   C#m7
Like a fool I went and stayed ____ too long.

E*   C#m7
Now I'm wond'rin' if your love's still ____ strong.

A
Ooh, ba - by, here I am,

A/B   E E7 E6 E5 Esus4 E*
Signed, sealed, delivered, I'm yours.   Mm.

Verse 2
E*   C#m7
Then that time I went and said ____ goodbye,

E*   C#m7
Now I'm back and not ashamed to cry.

A
Ooh, ba - by, here I am,

A/B   E*
Signed, sealed, delivered, I'm yours. ____ Ah.

Chorus 1

             E*   **E7***
Here I am ___ baby,   woh.

A   **A/B**   **E* E7***
You got my future in your hands.   Ah.

 A   **A/B**   **E**   **E7**
(Signed, sealed, de - livered, I'm yours.)

 A   **A/B** **E***   **E7***
 Here I am, baby,   ah,

A   **A/B**   **E* E7***
You got my future in your hands.   Hey.

 A   **A/B**   **E**   **E7**
(Signed, sealed, de - livered, I'm yours.)

 A   **A/B**
 I've done a lot of foolish things

E **E7**   **E6**   **E5**   **Esus4 E***
 That I really did - n't mean.   Ah, hey.

E   **E7 E6**   **E5 Esus4 E***
 Yeah, yeah,   didn't I?   Oh, __ baby.

Verse 3

E*   **C♯m7**
 Seen a lot of things in this ___ old world, (Ooh.)

E*   **C♯m7**
 When I touch the baby, baby girl.

    A
Ooh, ba - by, here I am,

A/B   **E** **E7 E6 E5**   **Esus4 E***
Signed, sealed, delivered, I'm yours.   I'm yours.

Verse 4

E*   **C♯m7**
 Oohee, baby, set my soul ___ on fire, (Ooh.)

     E*   **C♯m7**
That's ___why I know you're my only, on - ly desire.

    A
Ooh, ba - by, here I am,

A/B   **E***
Signed, sealed, delivered, I'm yours.

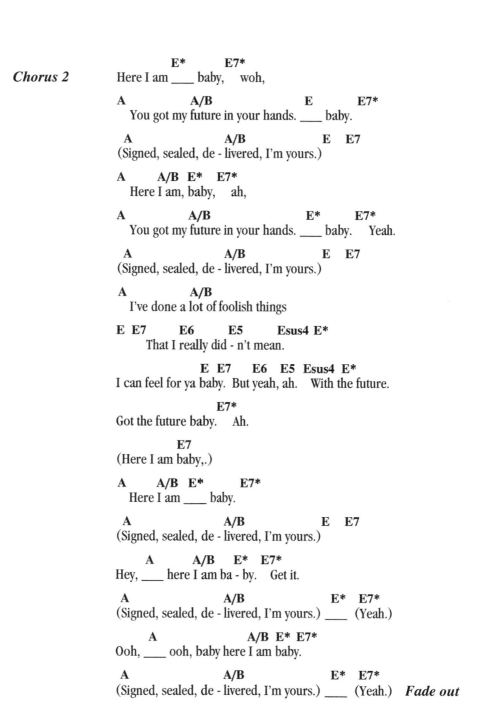

Chorus 2

       E*   E7*
Here I am ___ baby,   woh,

A   A/B   E   E7*
  You got my future in your hands. ___ baby.

A   A/B   E   E7
(Signed, sealed, de - livered, I'm yours.)

A   A/B E* E7*
  Here I am, baby,   ah,

A   A/B   E*   E7*
  You got my future in your hands. ___ baby.   Yeah.

A   A/B   E   E7
(Signed, sealed, de - livered, I'm yours.)

A   A/B
  I've done a lot of foolish things

E E7   E6   E5   Esus4 E*
  That I really did - n't mean.

                  E E7   E6   E5 Esus4 E*
I can feel for ya baby. But yeah, ah.   With the future.

              E7*
Got the future baby.   Ah.

          E7
(Here I am baby,.)

A   A/B E*   E7*
  Here I am ___ baby.

A   A/B   E   E7
(Signed, sealed, de - livered, I'm yours.)

     A   A/B   E*   E7*
Hey, ___ here I am ba - by.   Get it.

A   A/B   E*   E7*
(Signed, sealed, de - livered, I'm yours.) ___ (Yeah.)

      A   A/B E* E7*
Ooh, ___ ooh, baby here I am baby.

A   A/B   E*   E7*
(Signed, sealed, de - livered, I'm yours.) ___ (Yeah.)   *Fade out*

Sir Duke

Words and Music by
Stevie Wonder

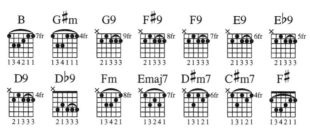

Music is a world with - in it - self _

Intro

‖: N.C. | | | :‖

Verse 1

  B   G#m
Music is a world with - in itself

      G9   F#9
With a language we all understand,

  B   G#m
With an equal opportu - nity

      G9   F#9 F9
For all to sing, dance and clap their hands.

Pre-Chorus 1

               E9   Eb9   D9   Db9
But just be - cause a record has a groove,

     D9   Eb9 E9
Don't make it in the groove.

                 Eb9   D9   Db9
But you can tell right a - way at let - ter A

        D9 Eb9 E9 F9 F#9
When the peo - ple start to move.

Chorus 1

  B   Fm
They can feel it all over.

Emaj7   D#m7 C#m7 F#
They can feel it all   over   people.

  B   Fm
They can feel it all over.

Emaj7   D#m7 C#m7 F#
They can feel it all   over, people go!

Interlude 1   ‖: N.C. | | | :‖

Verse 2

B   **G♯m**
Music knows it is and always will be

      G9   **F♯9**
One of the things that life just won't quit.

B   **G♯m**
But here are some of music's pioneers

           G9   **F♯9**   **F9**
That time will not allow us to forget, ___ now.

Pre-Chorus 2

           E9   **E♭9**   **D9**   **D♭9**
For there's Basie, Miller, Satchmo,

          D9   **E♭9**   **E9**
And the king of all, Sir   Duke.

                E♭9   **D9**   **D♭9**
And with a voice like Ella's ring - ing out,

           D9   **E♭9**   **E9**   **F9**   **F♯9**
There's no way the   band could lose.

Chorus 2

   B   **Fm**
‖:   You can feel it all over.

Emaj7   **D♯m7**   **C♯m7**   **F♯**
You can feel it all   over   people. :‖   *Play 3 times*

B   **Fm**
You can feel it all over.

Emaj7   **D♯m7**   **C♯m7**   **F♯**
You can feel it all   over me,   yeah, go, go!

Interlude 2   *Repeat Interlude 1*

Chorus 3

   B   **Fm**
‖:   You can feel it all over.

Emaj7   **D♯m7**   **C♯m7**   **F♯**
You can feel it all   over   people. :‖   *Play 5 times*

B   **Fm**
You can feel it all over.

Emaj7   **D♯m7**   **C♯m7**   **F♯**
Ev'rybody all   over,   people go!

Outro   *Repeat Interlude 1*

Someday We'll Be Together

Words and Music by Jackey Beavers,
Johnny Bristol and Harvey Fuqua

Melody:

Some - day we'll be to - geth - er.

(Capo 1st fret)

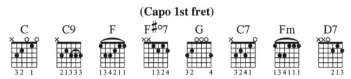

C   C9   F   F#°7   G   C7   Fm   D7

Intro	N.C.(C)			
	C			C9
	F		F#°7	

Chorus 1

    C   G   F   C
Some - day we'll be to - geth - er. Say it, say it, say it, say it again.

(You tell 'em.)

       G   F   C
Some - day we'll be to - gether. Oh yeah, oh, yeah.

Verse 1

    C
You're far away from me, my love. (Sing it pretty.)

 F   F#°7
And just as sure, my, my baby,   as there are stars above

Wanna say it, wanna say, wanna say it.

Chorus 2

    C   G   F   C
(Some - day we'll be to - geth - er.) Yes, we will. Yes, we will.

       G   F   C
(Some - day we'll be to - geth - er.)

I know, I know, I know, I know, I know.

Verse 2

C
My love is yours, baby, oh, right from the start.

F
(Sing it, hon - ey.)

F#°7
You, you, you, possess my soul now, honey.

And I know, I know you own my heart.

And I wanna say it.

Chorus 3

C   G   F   C
(Some - day we'll be to - geth - er.) Yes, we will. Yes, we will.

       G   F   C
(Some - day we'll be to - geth - er.) Yes, we will. Yes, we will.

Bridge

F
A long time ago, my, my sweet thing,

I made a big mistake, honey.

C
I, say I, said goodbye.

   C7   F
Oh, ___ oh, ba - by.

                         Fm
Ever, ever and ever and ever and ever,

Ever since that day now, now

   D7   G   N.C.
All ___ I , all I wanna do oh, is cry, ___ cry, cry. Hey, hey, hey.

Verse 3

C
I long for you every, ev'ry night.

F   F#°7
Just to kiss your sweet, sweet lips, baby.

Hold you ever, ever so tight.

And I wanna say it.

Outro

Repeat Chorus 3 till fade w/ vocal ad lib.

Standing in the Shadows of Love

Words and Music by Edward Holland,
Lamont Dozier and Brian Holland

Melody:

Stand-ing in the sha-dows of love, —

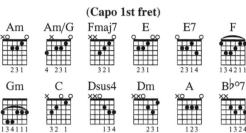

(Capo 1st fret)

Am   Am/G   Fmaj7   E   E7   F

Gm   C   Dsus4   Dm   A   Bb°7

Chorus 1	**Am** **Am/G** Standing in the shadows of love,

             Fmaj7   **E**   **E7**
I'm getting ready for the heartaches to come.

                    Am   **Am/G**
Can't you see me standing in the shadows of love?

             Fmaj7   **E**   **E7**
I'm getting ready for the heartaches to come.

Verse 1

               F   **Gm**   **C**
I want to run but there's nowhere to go.

          F   **Gm C**
'Cause heartaches will follow me I know.

                   F   **Gm**   **C**
Without your love, ___ the love ___ I need,

                  F   **Gm**   **C**
It's the begin - ning of the end   for me.

Dsus4   **Dm**
'Cause you've taken away   all my reasons for livin'

          A   **Bb°7**
When you pushed aside all the love I've been giving.

Now wait a minute.

Pre-Chorus 1

N.C.
Didn't I treat you right now, baby, didn't I?

Didn't I do the best I could, now didn't I? So you don't leave me...

Chorus 2

Am   Am/G
Standing in the shadows of love,

          Fmaj7   E   E7
I'm getting ready for the heartaches to come.

            Am   Am/G
Don't you see me standing in the shadows of love?

            Fmaj7   E   E7
Tryin' my best to get ready for the heartaches to come.

Verse 2

F   Gm   C
All alone, I'm des - tined to be

          F   Gm C
With miser - y my only   company.

              F   Gm   C
It may come to - day, it might   come tomorrow.

          F   Gm C
But it's for sure, I ain't got   nothing but sorrow.

Dsus4   Dm
Now, don't your conscience kind of bother you?

          A   Bb°7
How can you watch me cry after all I've done for you?

Now hold on a minute.

Pre-Chorus 2

N.C.
Gave you all the love I had now didn't I?

When you needed me I was always there now wasn't I?

Verse 3

   F   **Gm** **C**
(Standing in the shad - ows of love,)

         F   **Gm**   **C**
(Getting read - y for the heart - aches to come.)

      F   **Gm**   **C**
I'm trying not to cry ___ out loud.

      F   **Gm**   **C**
You know cryin' *it ain't gonna help me now.*

   Dsus4 Dm
What did I do   to cause all this grief?

      A   **B°7**
Now what'd I say to make you wanna leave?

Now wait a minute.

Pre-Chorus 3

N.C.
Gave my heart and soul to you now didn't I?

And didn't I always treat you good, now didn't I?

Chorus 3

     Am   **Am/G**
‖: I'm standing in the shadows of love,

      Fmaj7   **E**   **E7**
I'm getting ready for the heartaches to come.

       Am   **Am/G**
Don't you see me standing in the shadows of love?

      Fmaj7
Tryin' my best to get ready

            E   **E7**
For the heartaches to come. :‖ *Repeat and fade*

Uptight
(Everything's Alright)

Words and Music by Stevie Wonder,
Sylvia Moy and Henry Cosby

Ba - by,   ev - 'ry-thing is all   right. _

(Capo 4th fret)

Intro

| N.C.(drums) | | | N.C.(A7) | | |
‖: A | G/A | A | G/A :‖

Chorus 1

A   G/A
Baby, ev - 'rything is all right.

A   G/A
Uptight, out ____ of sight.

A   G/A
Baby, ev - 'rything is all right.

A   G/A
Uptight, out ____ of sight.

Verse 1

         A   **G/A**
I'm a poor ___ man's son from across the   railroad tracks.

        A   **G/A**
On - ly shirt I own is hangin' on my back.

           A   **G/A**
But I'm ___ the envy of ev'ry single guy,

          A   **G/A**
Since I'm ___ the apple of my ___ girl's eye.

          A   **G/A**
When we go out steppin' on the town ___ for awhile,

        A   **G/A**
My mon - ey's slow and my suits ___ are out of style.

        A   **G/A**
But it's all right if my clothes aren't new,

       A   **G/A**
Out ___ of sight, because my heart is true.

Chorus 2

         A   **G/A**
She says, "Baby, ev - 'rything is all right.

A   **G/A**
Uptight, out ___ of sight.

  A   **G/A**
Ba - by, ev - 'rything is all right.

A   **G/A**
Uptight and clean ___ out of sight.

Interlude   ‖: A |G/A   :‖ *Play 4 times*

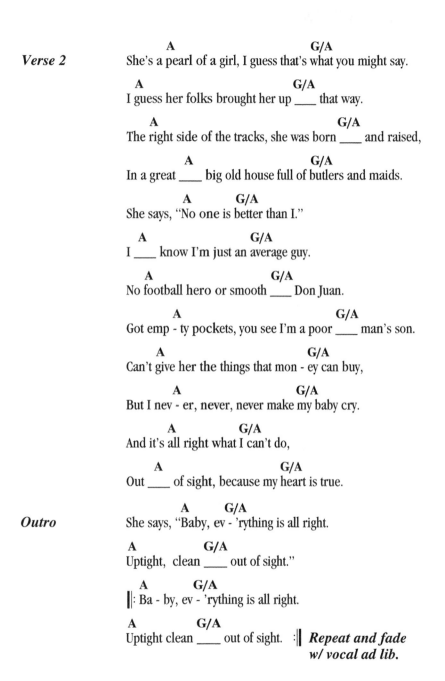

Verse 2

     A   G/A
She's a pearl of a girl, I guess that's what you might say.

  A   G/A
I guess her folks brought her up ___ that way.

      A   G/A
The right side of the tracks, she was born ___ and raised,

        A   G/A
In a great ___ big old house full of butlers and maids.

       A   G/A
She says, "No one is better than I."

  A   G/A
I ___ know I'm just an average guy.

  A   G/A
No football hero or smooth ___ Don Juan.

     A   G/A
Got emp - ty pockets, you see I'm a poor ___ man's son.

   A   G/A
Can't give her the things that mon - ey can buy,

     A   G/A
But I nev - er, never, never make my baby cry.

     A   G/A
And it's all right what I can't do,

   A   G/A
Out ___ of sight, because my heart is true.

Outro

     A   G/A
She says, "Baby, ev - 'rything is all right.

A   G/A
Uptight, clean ___ out of sight."

   A   G/A
‖: Ba - by, ev - 'rything is all right.

A   G/A
Uptight clean ___ out of sight. :‖ *Repeat and fade*
                                              w/ vocal ad lib.

Stop! In the Name of Love

Words and Music by Lamont Dozier,
Brian Holland and Edward Holland

Melody:

Stop! In the name of love,

Am   G/B   F   G   C   F/C   Cmaj7   Gm   A7   Fm7

Chorus 1

     Am   **G/B**
     Stop! In the name of love,

   F   **G**   **C F/C C**   **F/C C**
     Before you break my heart.

Verse 1

   C   **Cmaj7**
     Baby, baby, I'm a - ware of where you go

   Gm   **A7**
     Each time you leave my door.

   F   **G**
     I watch you walk down the street,

   F   **G**
     Knowing your other love you'll meet.

   C   **G/B**
     But this time before you run to her,

   F   **Fm**
     Leaving me a - lone and hurt,

         C   **F/C**   **C**
     (Think it over.)After I've been good to you.

          F/C   **C**
     (Think it over.)After I've been sweet to you.

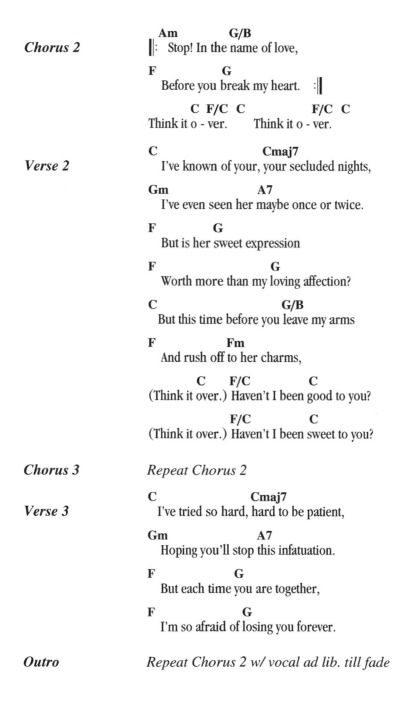

Chorus 2

Am   G/B

‖: Stop! In the name of love,

F   G

Before you break my heart. :‖

           C F/C C   F/C C

Think it o - ver.   Think it o - ver.

Verse 2

C   Cmaj7

I've known of your, your secluded nights,

Gm   A7

I've even seen her maybe once or twice.

F   G

But is her sweet expression

F   G

Worth more than my loving affection?

C   G/B

But this time before you leave my arms

F   Fm

And rush off to her charms,

        C   F/C   C

(Think it over.) Haven't I been good to you?

           F/C   C

(Think it over.) Haven't I been sweet to you?

Chorus 3   *Repeat Chorus 2*

Verse 3

C   Cmaj7

I've tried so hard, hard to be patient,

Gm   A7

Hoping you'll stop this infatuation.

F   G

But each time you are together,

F   G

I'm so afraid of losing you forever.

Outro   *Repeat Chorus 2 w/ vocal ad lib. till fade*

Superstition

Words and Music by
Stevie Wonder

Tune down 1/2 step:
(low to high) E♭ - A♭ - D♭ - G♭ - B♭ - E♭

Melody:

Ver - y su - per-sti - tious, _

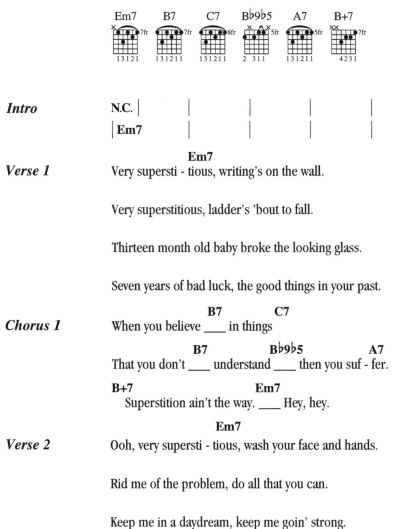

Em7   B7   C7   B♭9♭5   A7   B+7

Intro

N.C. | | | |

| Em7 | | | |

Verse 1

                  Em7
Very supersti - tious, writing's on the wall.

Very superstitious, ladder's 'bout to fall.

Thirteen month old baby broke the looking glass.

Seven years of bad luck, the good things in your past.

Chorus 1

                 B7   **C7**
When you believe ____ in things

             B7   **B♭9♭5**   **A7**
That you don't ____ understand ____ then you suf - fer.

B+7   **Em7**
  Superstition ain't the way. ____ Hey, hey.

Verse 2

                Em7
Ooh, very supersti - tious, wash your face and hands.

Rid me of the problem, do all that you can.

Keep me in a daydream, keep me goin' strong.

You don't wanna save me, sad is my song.

	B7 **C7**
Chorus 2	When you believe ____ in things

          B7   **B♭9♭5**   **A7**
You don't ____ understand ____ then you suf - fer.

B+7   **Em7**
Superstition ain't the way. ____ Hey, hey.

Interlude | **B7**   **C7** | **B7** **B♭9♭5** | **A7** | **B+7** |
                        | **Em7** | | | |

                        Em7
Verse 3   Very supersti - tious, nothing more to say.

Very superstitious, the devil's on his way.

Thirteen month old baby, mm, broke the looking glass.

Seven years of bad luck, good things in your past. Mm.

                        B7   **C7**
Chorus 3   When you believe ____ in things

                     B7   **B♭9♭5**   **A7**
That you don't ____ understand ____ and you suf - fer.

B+7   **Em7**
Superstition ain't the way. ____ No, no, no.

Outro   ‖: **Em7** | | | :‖ ***Repeat and fade***

Three Times a Lady

Words and Music by
Lionel Richie

Melody:

Thanks for the times that you've

(Capo 1st fret)

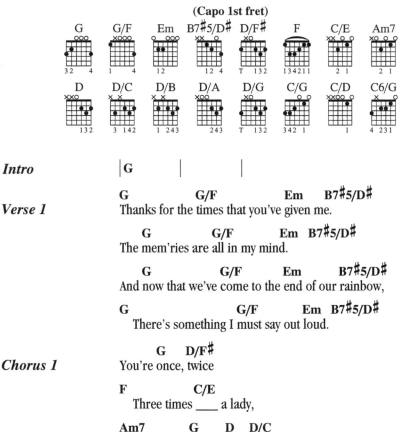

G G/F Em B7#5/D# D/F# F C/E Am7

D D/C D/B D/A D/G C/G C/D C6/G

Intro
| G | | |

Verse 1

       G   G/F   Em   B7#5/D#
Thanks for the times that you've given me.

          G   G/F   Em B7#5/D#
The mem'ries are all in my mind.

          G   G/F   Em   B7#5/D#
And now that we've come to the end of our rainbow,

    G   G/F   Em B7#5/D#
There's something I must say out loud.

Chorus 1

           G   D/F#
You're once, twice

      F   C/E
Three times ____ a lady,

  Am7   G   D   D/C
And I love ____ you.

            G   D/F#
Yes, you're once, ____ twice,

      F   C/E
Three times ____ a lady,

  Am7   G   D   D/C D/B
And I love ____ you.

        D/A G D/G C/G C/D
I love ____ you.

Verse 2

      G   **D/G**   **C6/G**   **C/D**
When we are to - gether, the moments I cherish

      G   **D/G**   **C6/G**   **C/D**
With ev'ry beat ____ of my ____ heart.

      G   **D/G**   **C6/G**   **C/D**
To touch you, to hold you, to feel you, to need you,

       G   **D/G**   **C6/G C/D**
There's nothing to keep us a - part.

Bridge

G	**D/G**	**C/G**	**C/D**	
G	**D/G**	**C/G**		
G	**D/G**	**C/G**		
G	**D/G**	**C/G**		

Chorus 2

C/G   **G**   **D/F♯**
  You're once, twice,

F   **C/E**
  Three times ____ a lady,

Am7   **G**   **D** **D/C** **D/B**
  And I love you,

     D/A **G**
I love ____ you.

The Tracks of My Tears

Words and Music by
William "Smokey" Robinson,
Warren Moore and Marvin Tarplin

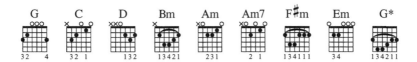

Peo-ple say I'm the life of the par - ty 'cause —

G C D Bm Am Am7 F#m Em G*

Intro

|G C | D |G C |Bm Am G |

　　　　　　　　　　　　　　　　　　　Do, do, do

　　　　　　C　　　　　　　D　　　　　　G
Doot.　Do, do, do, doot.　Do, do, do, ____ doot.

　　C　　　　　　　Bm　　Am　G
　Do, do, do, do,　do,　do.

Verse 1

　　　　G　　C　　　　　　　D
　　Peo-ple say I'm the life of the party

　　　　　　G　　　C　　　　　G Am7 G
'Cause ____ I tell a joke or two.

　　　　　　　　C　　　　　　　D
Although I might be laughin' loud and hearty,

G　　　C　　　　　G Am7 G
　Deep inside I'm blue.

Chorus 1

　　　　G　　C
So take a good ____ look at my face.

D　　　　　G　　C
　You'll see my smile ____ looks out of place.

　　　　G　　C
If you look closer it's easy

　　　　D　　　　　　　G　　C G Am7 G
To trace the tracks of my ____ tears

　　　　C　　G　　C　　G
I need you,　need you.

Verse 2

```
        C                      D
Since you left me, if you see me with another girl,

G        C              G  Am7  G
Seemin' like I'm havin' fun,

                    C                   D
Although she may be cute, she's just a substi-tute

        G        C              G  Am7  G
Because   you're the permanent one.
```

Chorus 2

```
G
So take a good look at my face.

D            G   C
  You'll see my smile ____ looks out of place.

            G      C
Look a little bit closer, it's easy

    D                G      C  G  Am7  G
To trace the tracks of my ____ tears.

    C   G     C   G
I need you,   need you.
```

Bridge

```
C   G        C      G    C   G          C   G
    Hey, hey, ____ yeah.   (Out-side)   I'm masquer-ading.

    C      G      C    G
(In-side,) my ____ hope is fading.

        C          G         C    G
(Just a clown,) ooh, yeah, since you put me down.

        F♯m  Em   G*   F♯m
My smile is    my   make-up

Em  G*  F♯m  Em  G*  F♯m  Em  D
I    wear since   my   break-up   with you.
```

Outro

```
            G        C
‖: Baby, take a Good ____ look at my face.

D            G   C
  You'll see my smile ____ looks out of place.

        D            G   C         D          G
Yeah, ____ just look clos - er, it's easy to trace the tracks of my tears,

C      G  Am7  G
Baby, ba-by, ba - by. :‖  *Repeat and fade*
```

The Way You Do the Things You Do

Words and Music by
William "Smokey" Robinson and Robert Rogers

Melody:

You got a smile so bright,

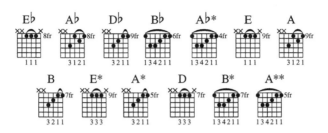

Intro

| Eb Ab Eb Ab | Eb Ab Eb Ab | Eb Ab Eb Ab |

Verse 1

Eb N.C.   Eb Ab Eb Ab
  You got a smile so bright,

Eb Ab   Eb   Ab   Eb Ab Eb Ab
  You know you could've been a can - dle.

Eb Ab   Eb Ab Eb Ab Eb Ab
  I'm holding you so   tight,

Eb Ab   Eb   Ab   Eb Ab Eb Ab
  You know you could've been a hand - le.

Eb Ab   Eb   Ab   Db Ab Db
  The way you swept me off my feet

Ab Db   Ab   Db   Eb Ab Eb Ab
  You know you could've been a broom.

Eb   Ab   Eb   Ab Eb Ab Eb Ab
  The way you smell so sweet,

Eb   Ab   Eb   Ab   Eb   Ab   Eb Ab Eb
  You know you could've been some per - fume.

	B♭ A♭*
Chorus 1	Well, you could've been anything that you wanted to

                       B♭ A♭*N.C.   E♭ A♭
And I can tell,   the way you do the things you do.

E♭   A♭   E♭ A♭ E♭ A♭
Ah, ____ ba - by.

Verse 2

E♭ N.C.   E♭ A♭ E♭ A♭
  As pretty as you are,

E♭   A♭   E♭   A♭   E♭   A♭ E♭ A♭
You know you could've been a flow - er.

E♭ A♭ E♭   A♭   E♭   A♭ E♭ A♭
If good looks caused a minute,

E♭   A♭   E♭   A♭ E♭ A♭ E♭ A♭
You know that you could be an hour.

E♭   A♭   E♭   A♭   D♭ A♭ D♭
The way you stole my heart.

A♭   D♭   A♭   D♭   E♭ A♭ E♭ A♭
You know you could've been a cool crook.

E♭   A♭ E♭   A♭ E♭ A♭ E♭ A♭
And, baby, you're so smart,

E♭   A♭   E♭   A♭   E♭   A♭   E♭ A♭ E♭
You know you could've been a school book.

Chorus 2

B♭   A♭*
Well, you could've been anything that you   wanted to

              B♭ A♭*N.C.   E♭ A♭
And I can tell,   the way you do the things you do.

E♭   A♭   E♭ A♭ E♭ A♭ E♭ N.C.
Ah, ____ ba - by.   Yeah.

Sax Solo	|E A E A |E A E A |E A E A |E A E A	
	|B E* B E* |A* D A* D |E A E A	

       E N.C.   E A E A

Verse 3   You made my life so rich,

       E   A   E   A   E   A E A

      You know you could have been some money.

       E   A   E   A E A E

      And baby, you're so sweet,

       E   A   E   A   E A E A E

      You know you could've been some honey.

       B*   A**

Chorus 3   Well, you could've been anything that you   wanted to

                   B* A** N.C.   E

      And I can tell,   the way you do the things you do.

          A   E   A   E

      (The way you do the things you do.)

          A   E   A   E   A   E   A   E

      You really swept me off ___ my feet. (The way you do the things you do.)

          A   E A E   A   E   A   E

      You made my life com - plete. (The way you do the things you do.)

          A   E A E   A   E   A   E

      You made my life so bright. (The way you do the things you do.)

           A   E A E

      ‖: You make me feel al - right.

          A   E   A   E

      (The way you do the things you do.) :‖ *Repeat and fade*

What Becomes of the Broken Hearted

Words and Music by James A. Dean,
Paul Riser and William Henry Weatherspoon

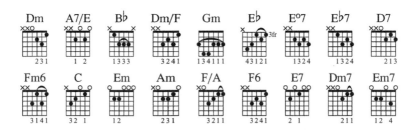

Intro	│ N.C. (F) │	│	│ **Dm A7/E** │
	│ **B♭** │	│ **Dm/F**	│ **Gm** │
	│ **E♭** │	│ **B♭**	│ **E°7** │
	│ **E♭** │	│ **Dm A7/E** │	

B♭   **Dm/F**

Verse 1   As I walk this land of broken dreams,

Gm   **E♭**
I have visions of many things.

B♭   **Dm/F**
But happiness is just an illusion

Gm   **D7**   **Fm6**
Filled with sadness and con - fusion.

Chorus 1

C   Em
   What becomes of the broken hearted

Am   F/A   F6
   Who had love that's now de - parted?

C   Em
I know I've got to find

Am   C
Some kind of peace of mind.

E7   F6 Gm E♭
Maybe.

Verse 2

B♭   Dm/F
   The roots of love grow all around,

Gm   E♭
   But for me they come a tumblin' down.

B♭   E°7
   Ev'ryday heartaches grow a little stronger,

E♭7   Dm7 A7/E
   I can't stand this pain much long - er.

B♭   Dm/F
   I walk in shadows, searching for light,

Gm   E♭
   Cold and alone no comfort in sight.

B♭   Dm/F
   Hoping and prayin' for someone who'll care,

Gm   Dm7   Fm6
   Always movin' and goin' no - where.

Chorus 2

C   Em
   What becomes of the broken hearted

Am   F/A   F6
   Who had love that's now de - parted?

C   Em
I know I've got to find

Am   C
Some kind of peace of mind.

E7   F6 Gm E♭
Help me, please.

Verse 3

B♭   **Dm/F**
I'm searching, though I don't succeed,

Gm   **E♭**
But someone look, there's a growin' need.

B♭   **E°7**
All is lost, there's no place for beginning.

E♭7   **Dm7 A7/E**
All that's left is an unhappy end - ing.

Chorus 3

B♭   **Dm/F**
Now what becomes of the broken hearted

Gm   **E♭**
Who had love that's now de - parted?

B♭   **Dm/F**
I know I've got to find some kind of peace of mind.

Gm   **E♭**
I'll be searching ev'rywhere just to find someone to care.

Outro

B♭   **Dm/F**
I'll be looking ev'ryday; I know I'm gonna find a way.

Gm   **E♭**
Nothing's gonna stop me now, I'll find a way somehow

B♭
I'll be searching ev'rywhere.   *Fade out*

What's Going On

Words and Music by Marvin Gaye,
Al Cleveland and Renaldo Benson

Melody:

Moth - er, moth - er, _   there's _too _ man-y

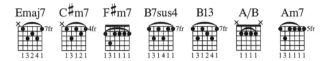

Emaj7 C#m7 F#m7 B7sus4 B13 A/B Am7

Intro |Emaj7 | | |

Verse 1
    Emaj7   **C#m7**
    Mother, mother, there's too many of you crying.

    Emaj7   **C#m7**
    Brother, brother, brother, there's far too many of you dying.

            F#m7
    You know we've got to find a way

            B7sus4   **B13**
    To bring some lovin' here today,   yeah.

Verse 2
    Emaj7   **C#m7**
    Father, father, we don't need to ___ escalate.

            Emaj7   **C#m7**
    You see war is not the answer, for only love can ___ conquer hate.

            F#m7
    You know we've got to find a way

            B7sus4   **B13**
    To bring some lovin' here today, ___ oh.

Pre-Chorus 1

      F#m7   A/B
Picket lines (Sister.) and picket signs (Sister.)

         F#m7   A/B
Don't punish me (Sister.) with bru - tality. (Sister.)

   F#m7   A/B
Talk to me, (Sister.) so you can see.

Chorus 1

B13   Emaj7   C#m7
   Oh, what's goin' on, what's goin' on?

            Emaj7   C#m7
Yeah, what's goin' on, oh, what's goin' on?

Interlude 1

‖: Am7 | | | :‖
w/ vocal ad lib.

| A/B | | | B13 |

Verse 3

Emaj7   C#m7
Mother, mother, ev'rybody thinks we're wrong.

    Emaj7   C#m7
Oh, but who are they to judge us simply 'cause our hair is long?

          F#m7
You know we've got to find a way

              B7sus4   B13
To bring some under - standin' here today, oh.

Pre-Chorus 2

F#m7   A/B
Picket lines (Brother.) and picket signs (Brother.)

    F#m7   A/B
Don't punish me (Brother.) with bru - tality. (Brother.)

      F#m7   A/B
Come on talk to me, (Brother.) so you can see.

Chorus 2

B13   Emaj7   C#m7
   Oh, what's goin' on, yeah, what's goin' on?

            Emaj7   C#m7
Tell me what's goin' on? I'll tell you what's goin' on.

Interlude 2   *Repeat Interlude 1*

Outro   ‖: Am7 | | | :‖ *Repeat and fade*
                                                 w/ vocal ad lib.

Where Did Our Love Go

Words and Music by Brian Holland,
Lamont Dozier and Edward Holland

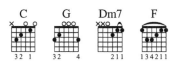

C	G	Dm7	F
32 1	32 4	2 1 1	1 3 4 2 1 1

Chorus 1

   C   G
Baby, baby, baby, don't leave me.

          Dm7   **G**
Ooh, please don't leave me all by myself.

Verse 1

 F   **C**   **G**
  I've got this burning, burning, yearning feeling in - side me.

       Dm7   **G**
Ooh, deep in - side me and it hurts so bad.

 F   **C**   **G**
  You came into my heart (Baby, baby.) so tender - ly

          Dm7
With the burning love ___ (Baby, baby.)

       G
That stings like a bee. (Baby, baby.)

 F   **C**   **G**
  Now that I sur - render (Baby, baby.) so helpless - ly.

       Dm7
You now want to leave. (Baby, baby.)

             G   **F**
Ooh, you wanna leave me. (Baby, baby.) Ooh. (Baby, baby.)

Chorus 2

    C   G   Dm7
Baby, baby, where did our love go? Ooh, don't you want me?

                      G   F
Don't you want me no more? (Baby, baby.) Ooh, baby.

Sax Solo

C		G		
Dm7		G	F	

Chorus 3

C   G
Baby, baby, where did our love go?

            Dm7   G
And all of your promises of a love forever - more. (Baby, baby.)

Verse 2

F   C   G
  I've got this burning, burning, yearning feelin' in - side me.

            Dm7   G
Ooh, deep in - side me (Baby, baby.) and it hurts so bad. (Baby, baby.)

F   C   G
  Before you won my heart, (Baby, baby.) you were a perfect guy.

            Dm7   G N.C.
But now that you got me, (Baby, baby.) you wanna leave me be - hind.

(Baby, baby.) Ooh, baby.

Outro

    C   G
‖: Baby, baby, baby, don't leave me.

            Dm7   G N.C.
Ooh, please don't leave me (Baby, baby.) all by my - self.

(Baby, baby.) Ooh. (Baby, baby.) :‖ *Repeat and fade*

You Are the Sunshine of My Life

Words and Music by
Stevie Wonder

Melody:

You are the sun - shine of ___ my _ life, ___

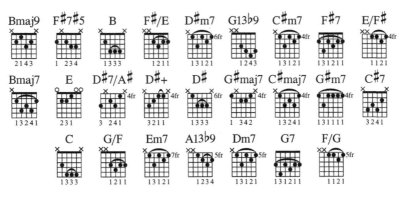

Intro	‖: Bmaj9 | |F#7#5 | :‖

Chorus 1

    B   **F#/E**   **D#m7 G13♭9**
    You are the sun - shine of my life,

    C#m7   **F#7**   **B C#m7 F#7**
    That's why I'll al - ways be around.

    B   **F#/E**   **D#m7 G13/9**
    You are the ap - ple of my eye.

    C#m7   **E/F#**   **B C#m7 F#7**
    Forever you'll ____ stay in my heart.

Verse 1

    B   **F#/E**   **E/F# Bmaj7**   **F#/E E/F#**
    I feel like this ____ is the ____ be - ginning,

    Bmaj7   **E**   **E/F#**   **D#7/A# D#m7 D#+ D#**
    'Though I've loved you for a mil - lion years.

    G#maj7 C#maj7   **D#**   **G#m7**
    And if I thought our love ____ was ____ ending,

        C#7   **F#7**
    I'd find ____ myself drowning in my own tears.

    Whoa, whoa.

Chorus 2

B   F#/E   D#m7 G13b9
You are the sun - shine of my life,

C#m7   F#7   B C#m7 F#7
That's why I'll al - ways stay around.

B   F#/E   D#m7 G13b9
You are the ap - ple of my eye.

C#m7   E/F#   B C#m7 F#7
Forever you ____ stay in my heart.

Verse 2

B   F#/E E/F# Bmaj7   F#/E E/F#
You must have known ____ that I ____ was ____ lonely,

Bmaj7   E   E/F#   D#7/A# D#m7 D#+ D#
Because you came ____ to my ____ rescue.

G#maj7 C#maj7   D#   G#m7
And I know that his must ____ be ____ heaven.

               C#7   F#7
How could so ____ much love be inside of you?

G7
Whoa,

Chorus 3

    C   G/F   Em7 A13b9
‖: You are the sun - shine of my life,

Dm7   G7   C Dm7 G7
That's why I'll al - ways stay around.

C   G/F   Em7 A13b9
You are the ap - ple of my eye.

Dm7   F/G   C Dm7 G7
Forever you ____ stay in my heart.   :‖ *Repeat and fade*

You Can't Hurry Love

Words and Music by Edward Holland,
Lamont Dozier and Brian Holland

I need love, love _____ to ease __ my mind.

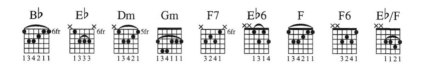

Bb	Eb	Dm	Gm	F7	Eb6	F	F6	Eb/F

Intro | N.C.(Bb) | | | |

Verse 1

Bb   **Eb**   **Bb**
    I need love, love to ease ____ my mind.

      Dm   **Gm**   **Eb**
    I need to find, find   someone to call ____ mine,

    F7
    But Mama said,

Chorus 1

      Bb   **Eb**   **Bb**
    "You can't hurry love. No, you just have to wait."

          Dm   **Gm**
    She said, "Love don't come easy,

    Eb   **F7**
    It's a game of give and take.

    Bb   **Eb**   **Bb**
    You can't hurry love. No, you just have to wait.

          Dm **Gm**   **Eb**   **F7**
    You've gotta trust, give it time, no matter how long ____ it takes."

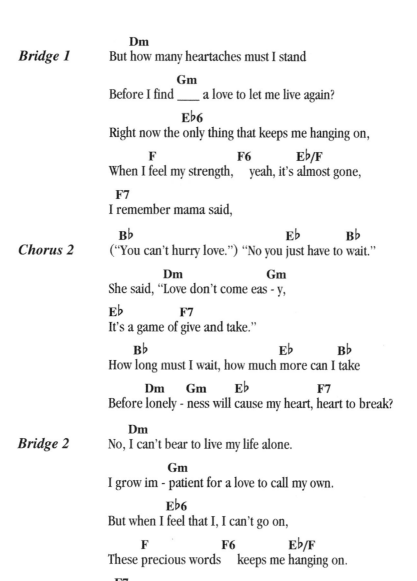

Bridge 1

Dm
But how many heartaches must I stand

      Gm
Before I find ____ a love to let me live again?

      E♭6
Right now the only thing that keeps me hanging on,

    F   F6   E♭/F
When I feel my strength,   yeah, it's almost gone,

F7
I remember mama said,

Chorus 2

   B♭   E♭   B♭
("You can't hurry love.") "No you just have to wait."

      Dm   Gm
She said, "Love don't come eas - y,

E♭   F7
It's a game of give and take."

   B♭   E♭   B♭
How long must I wait, how much more can I take

      Dm   Gm   E♭   F7
Before lonely - ness will cause my heart, heart to break?

Bridge 2

      Dm
No, I can't bear to live my life alone.

      Gm
I grow im - patient for a love to call my own.

      E♭6
But when I feel that I, I can't go on,

    F   F6   E♭/F
These precious words   keeps me hanging on.

  F7
I remember mama said,

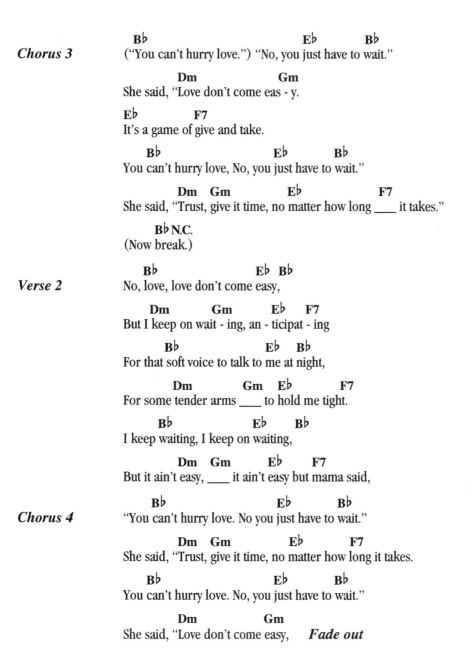

Chorus 3

  B♭   **E♭**   **B♭**
("You can't hurry love.") "No, you just have to wait."

        Dm   **Gm**
She said, "Love don't come eas - y.

E♭   **F7**
It's a game of give and take.

    B♭   **E♭**   **B♭**
You can't hurry love, No, you just have to wait."

        Dm   **Gm**   **E♭**   **F7**
She said, "Trust, give it time, no matter how long ____ it takes."

     B♭ N.C.
(Now break.)

Verse 2

    B♭   **E♭**   **B♭**
No, love, love don't come easy,

       Dm   **Gm**   **E♭**   **F7**
But I keep on wait - ing, an - ticipat - ing

     B♭   **E♭**   **B♭**
For that soft voice to talk to me at night,

       Dm   **Gm** **E♭**   **F7**
For some tender arms ____ to hold me tight.

    B♭   **E♭**   **B♭**
I keep waiting, I keep on waiting,

       Dm   **Gm**   **E♭**   **F7**
But it ain't easy, ____ it ain't easy but mama said,

Chorus 4

    B♭   **E♭**   **B♭**
"You can't hurry love. No you just have to wait."

       Dm   **Gm**   **E♭**   **F7**
She said, "Trust, give it time, no matter how long it takes.

    B♭   **E♭**   **B♭**
You can't hurry love. No, you just have to wait."

       Dm   **Gm**
She said, "Love don't come easy,   *Fade out*

You Keep Me Hangin' On

Words and Music by Edward Holland,
Lamont Dozier and Brian Holland

Melody:

Set me free why don't __you ba - by?

(Capo 1st fret)

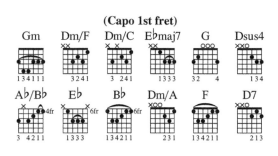

Gm   Dm/F   Dm/C   E♭maj7   G   Dsus4

A♭/B♭   E♭   B♭   Dm/A   F   D7

Intro

| Gm |Dm/F |Dm/C |E♭maj7 |

Chorus 1

G   Dm/F
   Set me free, why don't ____ cha baby?

Dm/C   E♭maj7   Dsus4
   Get out my life, why don't cha ba - by,

G   Dm/F
   'Cause you don't really love ____ me.

             Dm/C   E♭maj7   Dsus4
You just keep ____ me hangin' on.

G   Dm/F
   You don't really need ____ me,

              Dm/C   E♭maj7   Dsus4
But you keep ____ me hangin' on.

Verse 1

A♭/B♭   E♭   B♭
   Why do you keep comin' around playing with my heart?

A♭/B♭
   Why don't cha get out of my life,

E♭   B♭   Dm/A
   And let me make a new start?

F   D7
   Let me get over you the way you've gotten over me.

Chorus 2

G   Dm/F
Set me free, why don't ___ cha baby?

Dm/C   E♭maj7   Dsus4
Let me be, why don't ___ cha ba - by,

G   Dm/F
'Cause you don't really love ___ me.

          Dm/C   E♭maj7 Dsus4
You just keep ___ me hangin' on.

G   Dm/F
Now you don't really want ___ me,

          Dm/C   E♭maj7 Dsus4
You just keep ___ me hangin' on.

Verse 2

A♭/B♭   E♭   B♭
You say although we broke up you still wanna just be friends,

A♭/B♭
But how can we still be friends when

E♭   G
Seeing you only breaks my heart again?

N.C.
And there ain't nothin' I can do about it. Whoa, whoa, whoa.

Chorus 3

G   Dm/F
Set me free, why don't ___ cha baby?

Dm/C   E♭maj7   Dsus4
Get out my life, why don't ___ cha baby?

G   Dm/F
Set me free, why don't ___ cha baby?

Dm/C   E♭maj7   Dsus4
Get out my life, why don't ___ cha baby?

Verse 3

A♭/B♭
You claim you still care for me, but your

E♭   B♭
Heart and soul needs to be free.

A♭/B♭
Now that you've got your freedom

    E♭   B♭ Dm/A
You wanna still hold on to me.

F
You don't want me for yourself so

D7
Let me find somebody else. Hey, hey.

Chorus 4

G   Dm/F
Why don't cha be a man ___ about it,

Dm/C   E♭maj7 Dsus4
And set me free.

     G   Dm/F
Now,   you don't care a thing about me,

Dm/C   E♭maj7 Dsus4
You're just using me.

     G   Dm/F
Go on,   get out, get out - ta my life,

Dm/C   E♭maj7 Dsus4
And let me sleep at night.

G   Dm/F
'Cause you don't really love ___ me,

           Dm/C   E♭maj7 Dsus4
You just keep ___ me hanging on.   *Fade out*

You've Really Got a Hold on Me

Words and Music by
William "Smokey" Robinson

Melody:

I don't ___ like you, ___

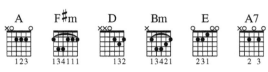

A	F#m	D	Bm	E	A7
1 2 3	1 3 4 1 1 1	1 3 2	1 3 4 2 1	2 3 1	2 3

Intro | A | F#m |

Verse 1

    A
I don't like you, but I love you.

F#m
Seems that I'm always thinking of you.

A   **D**
Oh, oh, oh, you treat me badly,

      Bm
I love you madly.

       E   **A**
You've really got a hold on me. (You've really got a hold on me.)

        F#m
You've really got a hold on me. (You've really got a hold on me.) Baby.

Verse 2

    A
I don't want you, but I need you.

F#m
Don't wanna kiss you, but I need to.

A   **D**
Oh, oh, oh, you do me wrong, now.

      Bm
My love is strong,now.

       E   **A**
You've really got a hold on me. (You've really got a hold on me.)

        F#m
You've really got a hold on me. (You've really got a hold on me.) Baby.

Bridge 1

A   A7   D
I love you and all I want you to do is just

A N.C. A N.C.
Hold me, hold me,

A N.C. E   N.C.   A
Hold me, hold me.

F#m E A
         Tighter.

F#m E A
         Tighter.

Verse 3

A
I wanna leave you, don't wanna stay here.

F#m
Don't wanna spend another day here.

A   D
Oh, oh, oh, I wanna split now;

       Bm
I just can't quit now.

      E   A
You've really got a hold on me. (You've really got a hold on me.)

         F#m
You've really got a hold on me. (You've really got a hold on me.) Baby.

Bridge 2

A   A7   D
I love you and all I want you to do is just

A N.C.   A N.C.
Hold me, (Please.) hold me, (Squeeze.)

A N.C. E   N.C.
Hold me, hold me.

Outro

     A
You've really got a hold on me. (You've really got a hold on me.)

     F#m   A
You've really got a hold on me. (You've really got a hold on me.)

Guitar Chord Songbooks

Each book includes complete lyrics, chord symbols, and guitar chord diagrams.

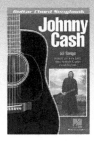 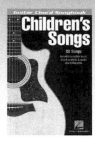  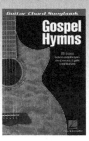 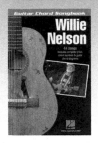

Acoustic Hits
More than 60 songs: Against the Wind • Name • One • Southern Cross • Take Me Home, Country Roads • Teardrops on My Guitar • Who'll Stop the Rain • Ziggy Stardust • and more.
00701787 ....$14.99

Acoustic Rock
80 acoustic favorites: Blackbird • Blowin' in the Wind • Layla • Maggie May • Me and Julio down by the Schoolyard • Pink Houses • and more.
00699540..................................$21.99

Alabama
50 of Alabama's best: Angels Among Us • The Closer You Get • If You're Gonna Play in Texas (You Gotta Have a Fiddle in the Band) • Mountain Music • When We Make Love • and more.
00699914..................................$14.95

The Beach Boys
59 favorites: California Girls • Don't Worry Baby • Fun, Fun, Fun • Good Vibrations • Help Me Rhonda • Wouldn't It Be Nice • dozens more!
00699566..................................$19.99

The Beatles
100 more Beatles hits: Lady Madonna • Let It Be • Ob-La-Di, Ob-La-Da • Paperback Writer • Revolution • Twist and Shout • When I'm Sixty-Four • and more.
00699562..................................$17.99

Bluegrass
Over 40 classics: Blue Moon of Kentucky • Foggy Mountain Top • High on a Mountain Top • Keep on the Sunny Side • Wabash Cannonball • The Wreck of the Old '97 • and more.
00702585..................................$14.99

Johnny Cash
58 Cash classics: A Boy Named Sue • Cry, Cry, Cry • Daddy Sang Bass • Folsom Prison Blues • I Walk the Line • Ring of Fire • Solitary Man • and more.
00699648..................................$17.99

Children's Songs
70 songs for kids: Alphabet Song • Bingo • The Candy Man • Eensy Weensy Spider • Puff the Magic Dragon • Twinkle, Twinkle Little Star • and more.
00699539..................................$16.99

Christmas Carols
80 Christmas carols: Angels We Have Heard on High • The Holly and the Ivy • I Saw Three Ships • Joy to the World • O Holy Night • and more.
00699536..................................$12.99

Christmas Songs
80 songs: All I Want for Christmas Is My Two Front Teeth • Baby, It's Cold Outside • Jingle Bell Rock • Mistletoe and Holly • Sleigh Ride • and more.
00119911..................................$14.99

Eric Clapton
75 of Slowhand's finest: I Shot the Sheriff • Knockin' on Heaven's Door • Layla • Strange Brew • Tears in Heaven • Wonderful Tonight • and more.
00699567 ....$19.99

Classic Rock
80 rock essentials: Beast of Burden • Cat Scratch Fever • Hot Blooded • Money • Rhiannon • Sweet Emotion • Walk on the Wild Side • and more.
00699598..................................$18.99

Coffeehouse Hits
57 singer-songwriter hits: Don't Know Why • Hallelujah • Meet Virginia • Steal My Kisses • Torn • Wonderwall • You Learn • and more.
00703318 ....$14.99

Country
80 country standards: Boot Scootin' Boogie • Crazy • Hey, Good Lookin' • Sixteen Tons • Through the Years • Your Cheatin' Heart • and more.
00699534 ....$17.99

Country Favorites
Over 60 songs: Achy Breaky Heart (Don't Tell My Heart) • Brand New Man • Gone Country • The Long Black Veil • Make the World Go Away • and more.
00700609 ....$14.99

Country Hits
40 classics: As Good As I Once Was • Before He Cheats • Cruise • Follow Your Arrow • God Gave Me You • The House That Built Me • Just a Kiss • Making Memories of Us • Need You Now • Your Man • and more.
00140859 ....$14.99

Country Standards
60 songs: By the Time I Get to Phoenix • El Paso • The Gambler • I Fall to Pieces • Jolene • King of the Road • Put Your Hand in the Hand • A Rainy Night in Georgia • and more.
00700608 ....$12.95

Cowboy Songs
Over 60 tunes: Back in the Saddle Again • Happy Trails • Home on the Range • Streets of Laredo • The Yellow Rose of Texas • and more.
00699636 ....$19.99

Creedence Clearwater Revival
34 CCR classics: Bad Moon Rising • Born on the Bayou • Down on the Corner • Fortunate Son • Up Around the Bend • and more.
00701786 ....$16.99

Jim Croce
37 tunes: Bad, Bad Leroy Brown • I Got a Name • I'll Have to Say I Love You in a Song • Operator (That's Not the Way It Feels) • Photographs and Memories • Time in a Bottle • You Don't Mess Around with Jim • and many more.
00148087 ....$14.99

Complete contents listings available online at www.halleonard.com

Crosby, Stills & Nash
37 hits: Chicago • Dark Star • Deja Vu • Marrakesh Express • Our House • Southern Cross • Suite: Judy Blue Eyes • Teach Your Children • and more.
00701609...............................$16.99

John Denver
50 favorites: Annie's Song • Leaving on a Jet Plane • Rocky Mountain High • Take Me Home, Country Roads • Thank God I'm a Country Boy • and more.
02501697 ....$17.99

Neil Diamond
50 songs: America • Cherry, Cherry • Cracklin' Rosie • Forever in Blue Jeans • I Am...I Said • Love on the Rocks • Song Sung Blue • Sweet Caroline • and dozens more!
00700606 ....$19.99

Disney
56 super Disney songs: Be Our Guest • Friend like Me • Hakuna Matata • It's a Small World • Under the Sea • A Whole New World • Zip-A-Dee-Doo-Dah • and more.
00701071 ....$17.99

The Doors
60 classics from the Doors: Break on Through to the Other Side • Hello, I Love You (Won't You Tell Me Your Name?) • Light My Fire • Love Her Madly • Riders on the Storm • Touch Me • and more.
00699888 ....$17.99

Eagles
40 familiar songs: Already Gone • Best of My Love • Desperado • Hotel California • Life in the Fast Lane • Peaceful Easy Feeling • Witchy Woman • more.
00122917 ....$16.99

Early Rock
80 classics: All I Have to Do Is Dream • Big Girls Don't Cry • Fever • Itsy Bitsy Teenie Weenie Yellow Polkadot Bikini • Let's Twist Again • Lollipop • and more.
00699916 ....$14.99

Folk Pop Rock
80 songs: American Pie • Dust in the Wind • Me and Bobby McGee • Somebody to Love • Time in a Bottle • and more.
00699651 ....$17.99

Folksongs
80 folk favorites: Aura Lee • Camptown Races • Danny Boy • Man of Constant Sorrow • Nobody Knows the Trouble I've Seen • and more.
00699541 ....$14.99

40 Easy Strumming Songs
Features 40 songs: Cat's in the Cradle • Daughter • Hey, Soul Sister • Homeward Bound • Take It Easy • Wild Horses • and more.
00115972 ....$16.99

Four Chord Songs
40 hit songs: Blowin' in the Wind • I Saw Her Standing There • Should I Stay or Should I Go • Stand by Me • Turn the Page • Wonderful Tonight • and more.
00701611 ....$14.99

Glee
50+ hits: Bad Romance • Beautiful • Dancing with Myself • Don't Stop Believin' • Imagine • Rehab • Teenage Dream • True Colors • and dozens more.
00702501 ....$14.99

Gospel Hymns
80 hymns: Amazing Grace • Give Me That Old Time Religion • I Love to Tell the Story • Shall We Gather at the River? • Wondrous Love • and more.
00700463 ....$14.99

Grand Ole Opry®
80 great songs: Abilene • Act Naturally • Country Boy • Crazy • Friends in Low Places • He Stopped Loving Her Today • Wings of a Dove • dozens more!
00699885 ....$16.95

Grateful Dead
30 favorites: Casey Jones • Friend of the Devil • High Time • Ramble on Rose • Ripple • Rosemary • Sugar Magnolia • Truckin' • Uncle John's Band • more.
00139461 ....$14.99

Green Day
34 faves: American Idiot • Basket Case • Boulevard of Broken Dreams • Good Riddance (Time of Your Life) • 21 Guns • Wake Me Up When September Ends • When I Come Around • and more.
00103074 ....$14.99

Irish Songs
45 Irish favorites: Danny Boy • Girl I Left Behind Me • Harrigan • I'll Tell Me Ma • The Irish Rover • My Wild Irish Rose • When Irish Eyes Are Smiling • and more!
00701044 ....$14.99

Michael Jackson
27 songs: Bad • Beat It • Billie Jean • Black or White (Rap Version) • Don't Stop 'Til You Get Enough • The Girl Is Mine • Man in the Mirror • Rock with You • Smooth Criminal • Thriller • more.
00137847 ....$14.99

Billy Joel
60 Billy Joel favorites: • It's Still Rock and Roll to Me • The Longest Time • Piano Man • She's Always a Woman • Uptown Girl • We Didn't Start the Fire • You May Be Right • and more.
00699632 ....$19.99

Elton John
60 songs: Bennie and the Jets • Candle in the Wind • Crocodile Rock • Goodbye Yellow Brick Road • Sad Songs Say So Much • Tiny Dancer • Your Song • more.
00699732 ....$15.99

Ray LaMontagne
20 songs: Empty • Gossip in the Grain • Hold You in My Arms • I Still Care for You • Jolene • Trouble • You Are the Best Thing • and more.
00130337...............................$12.99

Latin Songs
60 favorites: Bésame Mucho (Kiss Me Much) • The Girl from Ipanema (Garôta De Ipanema) • The Look of Love • So Nice (Summer Samba) • and more.
00700973 ....$14.99

Love Songs
65 romantic ditties: Baby, I'm-A Want You • Fields of Gold • Here, There and Everywhere • Let's Stay Together • Never My Love • The Way We Were • more!
00701043...............................$14.99

Bob Marley
36 songs: Buffalo Soldier • Get up Stand Up • I Shot the Sheriff • Is This Love • No Woman No Cry • One Love • Redemption Song • and more.
00701704...............................$17.99

Bruno Mars
15 hits: Count on Me • Grenade • If I Knew • Just the Way You Are • The Lazy Song • Locked Out of Heaven • Marry You • Treasure • When I Was Your Man • and more.
00125332 ....$12.99

Paul McCartney
60 from Sir Paul: Band on the Run • Jet • Let 'Em In • Maybe I'm Amazed • No More Lonely Nights • Say Say Say • Take It Away • With a Little Luck • and more!
00385035 ....$16.95

Steve Miller
33 hits: Dance Dance Dance • Jet Airliner • The Joker • Jungle Love • Rock'n Me • Serenade from the Stars • Swingtown • Take the Money and Run • and more.
00701146...............................$12.99

Modern Worship
80 modern worship favorites: All Because of Jesus • Amazed • Everlasting God • Happy Day • I Am Free • Jesus Messiah • and more.
00701801 ....$16.99

Motown
60 Motown masterpieces: ABC • Baby I Need Your Lovin' • I'll Be There • Stop! In the Name of Love • You Can't Hurry Love • and more.
00699734 ....$17.99

Willie Nelson
44 favorites: Always on My Mind • Beer for My Horses • Blue Skies • Georgia on My Mind • Help Me Make It Through the Night • On the Road Again • Whiskey River • and many more.
00148273 ....$17.99

Nirvana
40 songs: About a Girl • Come as You Are • Heart Shaped Box • The Man Who Sold the World • Smells like Teen Spirit • You Know You're Right • and more.
00699762 ....$16.99

Roy Orbison
38 songs: Blue Bayou • Oh, Pretty Woman • Only the Lonely (Know the Way I Feel) • Working for the Man • You Got It • and more.
00699752 ....$17.99

Peter, Paul & Mary
43 favorites: If I Had a Hammer (The Hammer Song) • Leaving on a Jet Plane • Puff the Magic Dragon • This Land Is Your Land • and more.
00103013...............................$19.99

Tom Petty
American Girl • Breakdown • Don't Do Me like That • Free Fallin' • Here Comes My Girl • Into the Great Wide Open • Mary Jane's Last Dance • Refugee • Runnin' Down a Dream • The Waiting • and more.
00699883 ....$15.99

Pink Floyd
30 songs: Another Brick in the Wall, Part 2 • Brain Damage • Breathe • Comfortably Numb • Hey You • Money • Mother • Run like Hell • Us and Them • Wish You Were Here • Young Lust • and many more.
00139116 ....$14.99

Pop/Rock
80 chart hits: Against All Odds • Come Sail Away • Every Breath You Take • Hurts So Good • Kokomo • More Than Words • Smooth • Summer of '69 • and more.
00699538 ....$16.99

Praise and Worship
80 favorites: Agnus Dei • He Is Exalted • I Could Sing of Your Love Forever • Lord, I Lift Your Name on High • More Precious Than Silver • Open the Eyes of My Heart • Shine, Jesus, Shine • and more.
00699634 ....$14.99

Elvis Presley
60 hits: All Shook Up • Blue Suede Shoes • Can't Help Falling in Love • Heartbreak Hotel • Hound Dog • Jailhouse Rock • Suspicious Minds • Viva Las Vegas • and more.
00699633 ....$17.99

Queen
40 hits: Bohemian Rhapsody • Crazy Little Thing Called Love • Fat Bottomed Girls • Killer Queen • Tie Your Mother Down • Under Pressure • You're My Best Friend • and more!
00702395 ....$14.99

Red Hot Chili Peppers
50 hits: Californication • Give It Away • Higher Ground • Love Rollercoaster • Scar Tissue • Suck My Kiss • Under the Bridge • and more.
00699710 ....$19.99

The Rolling Stones
35 hits: Angie • Beast of Burden • Fool to Cry • Happy • It's Only Rock 'N' Roll (But I Like It) • Miss You • Not Fade Away • Respectable • Rocks Off • Start Me Up • Time Is on My Side • Tumbling Dice • Waiting on a Friend • and more.
00137716 ....$17.99

Bob Seger
41 favorites: Against the Wind • Hollywood Nights • Katmandu • Like a Rock • Night Moves • Old Time Rock & Roll • You'll Accomp'ny Me • and more!
00701147 ....$12.99

Carly Simon
Nearly 40 classic hits, including: Anticipation • Haven't Got Time for the Pain • Jesse • Let the River Run • Nobody Does It Better • You're So Vain • and more.
00121011...............................$14.99

Sting
50 favorites from Sting and the Police: Don't Stand So Close to Me • Every Breath You Take • Fields of Gold • King of Pain • Message in a Bottle • Roxanne • and more.
00699921 ....$17.99

Taylor Swift
40 tunes: Back to December • Bad Blood • Blank Space • Fearless • Fifteen • I Knew You Were Trouble • Look What You Made Me Do • Love Story • Mean • Shake It Off • Speak Now • Wildest Dreams • and many more.
00263755...............................$16.99

Three Chord Acoustic Songs
30 acoustic songs: All Apologies • Blowin' in the Wind • Hold My Hand • Just the Way You Are • Ring of Fire • Shelter from the Storm • This Land Is Your Land • and more.
00123860 ....$14.99

Three Chord Songs
65 includes: All Right Now • La Bamba • Lay Down Sally • Mony, Mony • Rock Around the Clock • Rock This Town • Werewolves of London • You Are My Sunshine • and more.
00699720 ....$17.99

Two-Chord Songs
Nearly 60 songs: ABC • Brick House • Eleanor Rigby • Fever • Paperback Writer • Ramblin' Man Tulsa Time • When Love Comes to Town • and more.
00119236...............................$16.99

U2
40 U2 songs: Beautiful Day • Mysterious Ways • New Year's Day • One • Sunday Bloody Sunday • Walk On • Where the Streets Have No Name • With or Without You • and more.
00137744...............................$14.99

Hank Williams
68 classics: Cold, Cold Heart • Hey, Good Lookin' • Honky Tonk Blues • I'm a Long Gone Daddy • Jambalaya (On the Bayou) • Your Cheatin' Heart • and more.
00700607 ....$16.99

Stevie Wonder
40 of Stevie's best: For Once in My Life • Higher Ground • Isn't She Lovely • My Cherie Amour • Sir Duke • Superstition • Uptight (Everything's Alright) • Yester-Me, Yester-You, Yesterday • and more!
00120862 ....$14.99

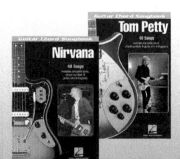

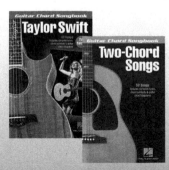